# TAKE BACK AMERICA

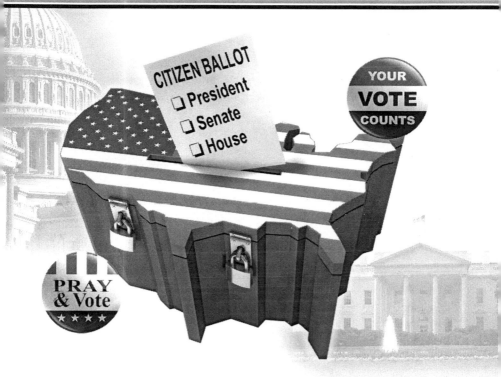

CITIZEN BALLOT

☐ President
☐ Senate
☐ House

YOUR VOTE COUNTS

PRAY & Vote
★ ★ ★ ★

# MATHEW D. STAVER

Foreword By The Late Dr. Jerry Falwell

New Revolution Publishers

# TAKE BACK
# AMERICA

By Mathew D. Staver

ISBN: 978-1-937102-00-5 Paperback

**Published by:**

New Revolution Publishers™
P.O. Box 540774
Orlando, Florida 32854
www.NewRevolutionPublishers.com
(800) 671-1776

First Printing, 2000
Second Printing, 2004
Third Printing, 2011

**Cover and Interior Design by:**
Heather Kirk
www.GraphicsByHeather.com

**Library of Congress Cataloging-in-Publication Data**
Staver, Mathew D., 1956-
    Take Back America/Mathew D. Staver
        p.   cm.
        1. Church and state – United States.  2. Freedom of religion – United States.
3. Religion in the public schools – Law and legislation – United States.  I. Title.
Library of Congress Card Number: 00-107778
ISBN 9781937102005

# TABLE OF CONTENTS

# ACKNOWLEDGMENTS

Since 1992, I have preached the essence of this book in various churches around the country. It is my hope that the message contained herein educates and motivates you as it has me.

I would like to thank Candy McGuire for her diligence in word processing and editing the updated version of this book. Despite a hectic schedule, Candy was able to keep this manuscript moving forward.

I would also like to thank my wonderful staff at Liberty Counsel. They are dedicated to the mission of restoring the culture.

Heather Kirk has designed the new, updated version of the cover and interior of my book. I greatly appreciate her dedication to this project.

Finally, I would like to thank my wife, Anita. She has been able to share my demanding schedule and perform her duties as President of Liberty Counsel, all at the same time. In the summer of 2002, she graduated from law school *summa cum laude* and received the honor of being named class valedictorian. Anita is not only my best friend, she is also my co-counsel and President of the organization we cofounded!

# FOREWORD

The very first time I met Mat Staver, I knew he was a man anointed by God for a very noble purpose: to protect and defend our constitutionally guaranteed religious freedoms.

Since forming Liberty Counsel in 1989 as a religious liberties education and legal defense organization, Mat has fulfilled his calling as a Christian attorney by defending our religious freedom with great success. Mat has been instrumental in a number of landmark cases before state courts, federal courts and even the United States Supreme Court. He defends the First Amendment rights of adults and children who are accused of nothing more than the free expression of their deeply held spiritual beliefs and values.

For many years Mat wrote a regular column dealing with religious freedom issues in my *National Liberty Journal*. He has also served on the Board of Trustees for Liberty University and as Chairman of the Steering Committee of Liberty University School of Law.

With the publication of *Take Back America*, Mat has struck a blow for the restoration of our cherished Judeo-Christian values that in recent years have been the target of an intolerant, irreligious minority.

It has become evident that we have neglected to maintain constant vigil over our religious freedoms. The withdrawal of faith-based citizens from the public square has emboldened the forces of darkness to declare that our values are no longer welcome. Now we face a tough fight to change the direction of our nation while we have the opportunity to do so.

America has forgotten its biblical roots. Children in public schools have in particular become targets of anti-Christian bigotry and legal terrorism under the guise of the so-called "separation of church and state," a practice Mat debunks as unconstitutional in itself.

Uncoupled from its biblical base, America has become a nation of uncurbed excesses. Night after night we see stories of violence and mayhem in our cities. Our schools have become war zones. Our entertainment serves to promote the basest impulses of society.

Such a time calls for people of God to once again turn to Him, instead of government, as the source of healing for our land. As Mat writes, "No form of government, republic or dictatorship, can restrain an unrestrained people."

The first step in taking back America is for Christians to take back their families. From that foundation we can strongly challenge the anti-God forces that have gripped our nation.

# Foreword

This well-documented and informative book is a valuable tool for parents, pastors, educators, business people and all citizens that care about the future of this great nation.

THE LATE DR. JERRY FALWELL,
Founder, Liberty University

*EDITOR'S NOTE: Dr. Falwell left this world to be with the Lord on May 15, 2007. Mat Staver had first met Dr. Falwell in the early 1990s and worked with him and Jerry Falwell Jr. to launch Liberty University School of Law. Mat currently serves as the Founder and Chairman of Liberty Counsel and Dean and Professor of Law at Liberty University School of Law.*

# PREFACE

In November of 1992, former Governor William Jefferson Clinton was elected as the forty-second President of the United States. As I searched for the reasons why someone of Mr. Clinton's "character" could become President of the United States, I realized that his rise to power was not the fault of Ross Perot diluting the popular vote, nor was the reason due to the politics of the Republican Party. The answers were deeper, and the reasons were more complex.

I was even more shocked when Barack Obama was elected president in 2008. America is generally right of center, but Obama represents the radical left of the political and social values spectrum. He is the most pro-abortion president in American history. How could America elect a president who is so far to the left of center?

I began reading the book of Deuteronomy. When I came to Chapter 28, I was astounded. The entire chapter read like a daily newspaper. I had read this chapter many times before, but this time something was different.

The theme of Deuteronomy is simple: If you obey God and keep His commandments, the nation will be blessed; if you disobey

God and His commandments, the nation will be cursed. The blessings and curses will affect every level of society, from the family to the farmer, from the city to the Commander-in-Chief.

In addition to reading the book of Deuteronomy, I have spent a lot of time reading the Declaration of Independence. The Declaration of Independence has become my favorite historical document. I encourage everyone to read the Declaration several times a year. The Declaration clearly sets forth the founders' understanding of the purpose and role of government.

Our nation was founded upon Christian principles of morality and virtue. These great principles were not separated from religion. They were inspired and undergirded by religion. The founding fathers presupposed that the people would be virtuous and self-restrained. Virtue and self-restraint would flow from religious values. This is not to say that all the early settlers were Christian, but they nevertheless operated from a general Christian worldview.

Over the past several decades, our country has become more and more secular. At the same time, the country has also become more splintered. Chaos has replaced order. Fear has replaced tranquility. In an effort to remedy the general breakdown of our society and the rising crime rate, Americans seem eager to give up their rights in exchange for a promise from government to protect them. Our elected officials promise more state and federal money, more programs, more police. These efforts to remedy societal ills are like putting a band-aid on cancer. While the band-aid might appear to fix the problem, underneath the cancer continues to spread.

# Preface

The message of Deuteronomy is straightforward. No amount of programs will put Humpty Dumpty back together again. Humpty Dumpty must be fixed from within. The founders understood this concept when they penned the Declaration of Independence. This great document is, in my opinion, the most powerful historical document of America. The founders understood that the Declaration was a "reflection of the American mind." More than any other document, it declares the purpose of government and the inspiration behind the American Revolution.

It is my desire that this book will inspire you to reflect on the messages of Deuteronomy and the Declaration of Independence. It is also my hope that you take seriously our precious freedoms, and that the messages of these two great documents will motivate you to reclaim the values and principles upon which this great country was founded.

MATHEW D. STAVER, B.A., M.A., J.D.
Founder and Chairman, Liberty Counsel
Dean, Liberty University School of Law
Chairman, Liberty Counsel Action

# INTRODUCTION
## The "Take Back America" Movement

I am entering the second decade of the new Millennium with great anticipation and excitement. While there are giants in the land and mountains in our path, I see God leading us forward! At Liberty Counsel, we worship the Mountain Mover and mountains simply don't intimidate us. This is a time to rebuild and begin moving forward, not a time to shrink back. The year 2011 and subsequent years will be known as our years because this is our time!

There can be no doubt that we will face many giants and sizeable challenges in the years ahead, including, at the time of this writing, a socialist United States Congress and the most pro-abortion President in the history of our nation.

Since 2009, President Barack Obama and the ultraliberal congressional leadership teamed up to fund abortion in the District of Columbia and around the world, pass Hate Crimes legislation, and flagrantly wave the banner of sexual perversion. But they did so at a very high political cost.

Barack Obama's ratings have dropped faster than any American President in history during his time in office. And

# TAKE BACK AMERICA

the "Obama Train" was derailed at the ballot box in November 2009 in several off-year elections, most notably in Virginia and New Jersey. Then, 2010's historic midterm elections completely repudiated the "Obama agenda."

The majority of Americans are beginning to stand up to the attempted "remaking of America" as evidenced by the confrontational "Town Hall" meetings held in 2009 and 2010, several massive, impromptu "Tea Party" protest meetings, the free-fall of the President's and Congress's approval ratings, and the historic crumbling of the ultraliberal 111th Congress. The signals couldn't be more clear: it is time to Take Back America!

## Government Healthcare Threatens Life and Liberty

The healthcare "reform" legislation known as ObamaCare is overtly unconstitutional.

Congress does not have unlimited authority to regulate private actions. If the Constitution does not give Congress the power to act, then Congress cannot act. Congress clearly lacks the constitutional authority to force individuals to have — or businesses to provide — health insurance. Congress's attempt to force health insurance coverage on the nation is a stunning example of what Congress cannot do under the Constitution of the United States of America!

If Congress had the power to force Americans to buy health insurance, then individual liberty would be overpowered and thus become meaningless. No matter what certain elected officials may desire, there are some things Congress simply cannot do.

The healthcare bills passed by the House of Representatives and the Senate in 2009 and 2010 are unconstitutional because Congress lacks the authority to mandate insurance coverage for individuals or private businesses. When a final bill passed in March 2010 that mandated such coverage, Liberty Counsel immediately filed suit against it!

The government healthcare bill funds abortion and measures the value of life on a cost-benefit scale. I don't want a government bureaucrat in Washington, DC, telling my aging relatives that their lives are not worth the cost of their annual healthcare. I don't want to fund abortion. Nor do I want some government agent to counsel families on "increasing the interval between pregnancies."

ObamaCare will become a "poison pill" to America as we know her and to our liberties that we love. Government is the least efficient system possible when it intrudes into the province of free enterprise. I don't want my medical choices placed in the hands of political power brokers and career politicians. The stakes of the ongoing battle for life and liberty have been raised by the Obama/Reid power axis, and we are rising to the challenge.

What do you call it when a radical minority forces its will on the law-abiding majority? The Obama/Reid power axis would have us call it "progressive leadership." The Founders called it "tyranny."

At every step of the way in ObamaCare's long march through Congress, the liberal Democrat leaders used trickery and overt manipulation to thwart the American people's legitimate concerns about the socialist takeover of our medical system.

Our Constitution has been subverted right before our eyes!

The "checks and balances" our Founders gave us are being overpowered and dismantled by the Obama/Reid power axis. Never before has the clear will of the people been so completely ignored and marginalized.

That's why Liberty Counsel filed suit in federal court challenging the bill's constitutionality!

Together, we are restoring the principle Truth enshrined in the Declaration of Independence — that Life, Liberty, and the Pursuit of Happiness are God-given, unalienable rights.

## A Surreal Experience on National Constitution Day

It was September 17, 2009, and I was sitting at counsel's table in a federal court in Pensacola, Florida. Two hundred and twenty-two years ago on September 17, 1787, the delegates of the Thirteen Colonies gathered in Philadelphia at Independence Hall to sign the Constitution of the United States of America.

In the courtroom to my left hanging on the wall was a large painting depicting that epic day. To my right was Robert Freeman, the Athletic Director for Pace High School in Santa Rosa County with forty years of service in the school system. To his right sat the Principal, Frank Lay, who had thirty years of service and who had planned on retiring in 2010. To the right of Frank Lay sat Harry Mihet, Senior Litigation Counsel for Liberty Counsel.

My eyes scanned the court chambers and my mind absorbed the moment. I thought of the crowds we walked through outside comprised of young and old who showed up to pray and offer their support for Frank and Robert. My mind was carried back to communist Romania where Harry was born and lived until 1990. Harry's dad was a pastor and missionaries smuggled Bibles to him to distribute to the people.

In the middle of the night Harry was jarred awake by the sound of secret police pounding on their front door. They had come with their German Shepherds to confiscate the forbidden Bibles. While Harry's dad greeted the police, Harry's mom went to the kitchen where the Bibles were stacked on the floor. She placed a piece of plywood on top of the Bibles and threw a cloth over the plywood. The makeshift tabletop was uneven, but it would have to do.

Harry's mom then brewed coffee brought to them by the same missionaries. Soon the aroma filled the room. She invited the secret police and their trained dogs into the kitchen where she offered the police the fresh coffee around the table. The communists were not fortunate to have good coffee, so these secret police were pleased to enjoy this delight. All the while they never suspected that under the table lie the very contraband they were sent to confiscate. After they finished enjoying the coffee, the secret police left and never found the Bibles.

I then thought about the events Harry experienced beginning on December 15, 1989, in his home town of Timisoara. On that date the police arrested Pastor Laszlo Tokes, who had recently made critical statements against the Romanian Communist Party to the Hungarian media. The government alleged he was inciting ethnic hatred. Parishioners soon gathered outside his house and would not disperse. The crowds grew larger and the people began to shout "Libertate" (Liberty) and "Exista Bumnezeu" (God exists). Eventually the entire town of several hundred thousand people showed up and they eventually knelt in one accord to recite the Lord's Prayer.

The dictator, Nicolae Ceausescu, called in the military to quell the growing protest, but the soldiers failed to restore order. The protests grew from Timisoara to other parts of Romania, including Bucharest. On December 21, Ceausescu tried to quell the crowds by addressing them with his usual communist propaganda and broadcasting his speech throughout Romania, but this time the people would have nothing to do with it. Panicked by the crowd's response, Ceausescu and his wife retreated inside the Central Committee Building where he had given his speech from the balcony.

Ceausescu's repressive regime collapsed soon thereafter. He was arrested and tried on December 25 by the Extraordinary Military Tribunal. After two hours, he was convicted and immediately executed. On Christmas Day, 1989, Harry Mihet experienced his first day of freedom!

As these thoughts rushed through my mind, the prosecutor whirled around, pointed his finger at Frank and Robert, raised his voice like a revivalist preacher, and urged the judge to throw the book at these criminals! The penalty for their "crimes" was six months in jail, a $5,000 fine, and the possible loss of their collective 70 years of retirement benefits.

But, what was their crime? Why were we in court in the first place? It all began when the American Civil Liberties Union (ACLU) embarked on a 335 million dollar fundraising campaign, which the group successfully achieved in 2008. In a press release, the ACLU boasted that it was going to use the new money to put more boots on the ground in several key states, including Florida. Soon thereafter the ACLU filed suit against the Santa Rosa County School Board, seeking to suppress all religious freedom in the district.

The ACLU then obtained an injunction from a federal court and later negotiated a Consent Decree from the school district that was approved by a federal judge as an enforceable order. The breadth of these orders are shocking, even prohibiting religious expression off campus on private time (a constitutional impossibility but nevertheless such was ordered by the court).

After one of these orders was entered, Frank and Robert were hosting a lunch for about 18 people to thank them for contributing to a new athletic facility. Before the lunch, and while no students were in the small room, Frank turned to Robert and asked him to bless the meal, which he did. When the ACLU learned of this "crime," they informed the judge and urged the court to pursue civil and criminal sanctions against them.

As I sat in court that day, the entire scene was surreal. I had been defending religious liberties for 20 years at that time and I had never experienced a day like this one. Is this really America? Can this be happening in my country? Was this a fanciful reenactment of what might be? No! This was really happening – on Constitution

Day of all days! The kaleidoscope of information from the past merged with the reality of that day to give me an out-of-body like experience as though I was observing all this from afar.

I quickly had to snap back to reality of the courtroom because my clients' future was on the line. After an all day trial, the judge gave the verdict in the late evening of "Not guilty!" When the crowds outside heard the verdict, they erupted in cheers. We won! But, we should have never been in court in the first place.

This is not the America envisioned by the Founders. This is not my America. It is time to take back America before it is too late.

I never want to experience another day like the one on September 17, 2009.

It is time to take back America! In one accord, we must draw a line in the sand. May our actions today bless future generations.

## Why We Must Confront the ACLU at Every Turn

Thanks to the ACLU, this is no longer the America our Founders envisioned, but when we aggressively stand against them, we almost always win!

Here's another encouraging story to illustrate the vulnerability of the ACLU. It involves Megan Chapman, a godly young woman who courageously stood up to the ACLU when it sued her high school in Kentucky to stop her from praying at her 2006 graduation ceremony. Just a few hours before the commencement, we were able to reach Megan by telephone. I assured her we could get the federal court's order overturned and that Liberty Counsel would stand by her.

After the graduation ceremony began a few hours later, the entire senior class stood up and recited the Lord's Prayer in unison! Then Megan approached the podium. Instead of a prayer, she shared her personal testimony amidst repeated applause from the audience. The Louisville *Courier–Journal* reported the next day that a "revival-like atmosphere" broke out during the graduation ceremony!

Megan and I then appeared on Fox News that evening. Later, Megan and her twin sister, Mandy, appeared on CNN's full-length documentary "God's Christian Warriors," that has been aired repeatedly around the world. Millions of people have now seen their bold testimony for Jesus!

Megan graduated from Liberty University in May 2010. I had the great pleasure of signing her acceptance letter to Liberty University School of Law, where she has begun her legal studies.

Instead of silencing a young high school girl through its outrageous intimidation tactics, the ACLU inspired a Champion for Christ who will join us in the legal arena to fight for life, liberty, and family! God will not be mocked. He will always turn apparent adversity into opportunity if we are faithful.

## We Are Not Shrinking Back in These Challenging Times — We Are Pressing Forward!

Liberty Counsel is poised to make a difference in the courtrooms, in the halls of Congress, and in the classrooms of America. With our unique relationship to Liberty University School of Law and the founding of Liberty Counsel Action, we are aggressively

# TAKE BACK AMERICA

"Raising Liberty to a Higher Power." The combination of the largest evangelical university in the world with a premier public interest law firm and a powerful grassroots advocacy organization gives us unprecedented weapons with which to win the war for American culture!

And through our key role in bringing forth the Freedom Federation, Liberty Counsel is working with the nation's largest faith-based and policy organizations to mobilize a Movement to literally "Take Back America."

I have gone on record as saying that this will be recognized as one of the most exciting times in our nation's history. While there may be giants in the land and extraordinary mountains to climb, I refuse to get fixated on them. Rather, I see the God of Abraham, Isaac, and Jacob, who towers over the giants and who made the mountains! I see opportunity, not adversity. I see a God who works miracles and with whom nothing is impossible.

This is *our* time because it is *God's* time!

Commit yourself, your family, and your friends to pray for the nation we all love. Together, we can take back the ground that has been stolen!

God is eager to work miracles through each one of us, even as He has in Megan Chapman's life. He has worked miracles in the past. He is the same yesterday, today, and forever!

Let's rejoice together as we rebuild the foundations of our nation. Let's move forward and take back the ground stolen by the ACLU and other anti-faith, anti-American groups. Again, this is *our* time…and this is *our* America!

# CHAPTER 1
## America at the Crossroads:
### *Which Vision of the Future Will We Choose?*

Liberty Counsel has a vision for America and our future, and so does the American Civil Liberties Union (ACLU). Those visions are as different as night and day. In fact, they are so diametrically opposed that they can be seen as representing a struggle of polar opposites. Which future will prevail depends on you and me. The future our children and grandchildren will experience rests upon our prayers and actions at this crucial hour.

The future envisioned by the ACLU is clearly illustrated through its body of litigation. Take, for instance, the Mojave Desert Cross case, officially known as *Salazar v. Buono*, which was heard at the United States Supreme Court. Erected in the middle of a desert in 1934 as a memorial to fallen World War I veterans, the ACLU wanted the cross removed after it had been in place for 75 years without any controversy. One has to drive for hours into the California desert to even lay eyes on this memorial.

After the ACLU sued, the court ordered the cross to be covered by a canvas tarp tied at its base. Congress then moved to try to save the cross, by proposing that the ground upon which it was erected be given to the Veterans of Foreign Wars in exchange for the donation of an equivalent piece of land to the federal government. The ACLU responded to this reasonable solution by saying, "No way, the cross must go!"

While the case was moving toward consideration at the Supreme Court, the canvas covering that was designed to hide the cross was buffeted by strong desert winds until it hung on the cross in tatters. The once-again visible cross was then boarded up with square plywood on both sides, so it looked like a blank billboard!

Liberty Counsel filed an extensive *amicus* brief with the Supreme Court, calling for the memorial to remain. When the Washington Press Corps gathered on the front steps of the High Court to interview participating parties after the hearing in early October 2009, Mandi Campbell, our Legal Director for the Liberty Center for Law and Policy, spoke on Liberty Counsel's behalf. Mandi is a 2009 graduate of Liberty University School of Law and is part of the new generation we are training to take on groups which attack our nation's heritage of Christian liberty. Our vision for the future includes training and equipping large numbers of young men and women to continue defending religious liberty, as long as it is attacked by misguided adversaries like the ACLU!

The visions of the ACLU and Liberty Counsel could not contrast more sharply, as illustrated by the Mojave Desert Cross case. The ACLU wants to remove God and any memory of Him from America. We, on the other hand, believe that America was founded upon a reverence for God and His Word that must be protected at all costs.

Liberty Counsel joins George Washington and the entire founding generation in boldly proclaiming that the twin pillars upon which America was established are religion and morality. Remove these pillars and America will surely collapse!

On another front, I argued at the Sixth Circuit Federal Court of Appeals in 2009 against the ACLU's bigotry concerning a public display of the Ten Commandments. A "Foundations of American Law and Government" display in Kentucky showed the Commandments surrounded by nine equal-sized, framed documents illustrating the development of American law, but the ACLU has singled out the Ten Commandments for elimination from historical consideration!

I have a different recollection of America's legal history. The Ten Commandments profoundly influenced American law and our understanding of right and wrong. The ACLU wants us to forget that history. It has a different vision of both our past and our future! In fact, the ACLU envisions an America completely devoid of any reference to God whatsoever. Liberty Counsel has a very different vision.

Also, in 2008, I argued at the California Supreme Court and at a Federal Court of Appeals in California against the ACLU regarding the definition of marriage. I believe marriage is the union of one man and one woman. The Bible is clear on this matter, and common sense leaves no room for doubt. But the ACLU's vision of the future is vastly different and makes no reference to either common sense or God's Word.

# TAKE BACK AMERICA

## We Will Get the Future for Which We Decide to Fight

What vision for America and for our children do you hold? The struggle we face today has very distinct sides: good against evil, freedom versus oppression, life against death. Whether we choose to engage in the battle or not, the war will rage on. One vision of America will win ... and one will lose.

As for me and my household (and that certainly includes Liberty Counsel), we will serve the Lord. The gift of liberty we have inherited is too precious to squander. It is our God-ordained duty to fight for what is right and good and was obtained and preserved at a great price.

A friend of mine shared a story with me of something that happened on a visit to the Holocaust Museum in Jerusalem. An unfamiliar lady approached him and asked if he was a Jew. He is a Jewish Christian, so he informed her of that fact.

Inexplicably, she began to weep. She then told him that as a young woman during the Holocaust years, she had lived within sight of Nazi incinerators. Each morning, she could smell the stench of burning flesh. As she sobbed, she said in a broken voice, "I did nothing. I am so very sorry — I did nothing."

May it never be said of Liberty Counsel — or any of our many friends and supporters — that we did nothing in our time of great moral challenge. Now is the time to pray and act! The future depends on what we do right now. Together, let's work to restore the foundations!

## Criminalizing Christianity

The ACLU has long distinguished itself as being America's leading "enemy within," but I have never seen their bullying result in criminal contempt charges being brought against citizens whose only "crime" was exercising their freedom of religion! Liberty Counsel's representation of Christian Educators Association International and school employees in Santa Rosa County, Florida, deals with a chilling new ACLU tactic that we are stopping so that it is not repeated in communities like yours. This story is so important that it bears retelling in greater detail.

"Shocked" is the best way to describe our reaction to comments made by a Florida federal judge. She would pursue civil contempt charges brought by the ACLU against a school district support staff and would refer two other public school officials to the U.S. Attorney's office to face *criminal* contempt charges!

And if the U.S. Attorney chose not to pursue criminal charges, Judge Casey Rogers said she would appoint a *Special Prosecutor* to pursue criminal contempt charges to the full extent possible!

What did these employees of the Santa Rosa County School District do to warrant this severe action by Judge Casey? Did they abuse children or commit some despicable crime against the public they were paid to serve?

No! They prayed — well, they didn't even personally pray. During an awards banquet at which Principal Frank Lay was present, his school's Athletic Director, Robert Freeman, prayed before the meal. At another event, Michelle Winkler's husband (who is not even employed by the school district) prayed over a meal at a privately sponsored event in a neighboring county, where other staff members were present.

Liberty Counsel came to the defense of Frank, Robert, and Michelle, all of whom are godly staff members working at Pace High School in Northern Florida. Some months earlier, the district was sued by the ACLU for allegedly allowing religious activities on campus. Judge Casey signed an order drafted by the ACLU, which essentially *banned all employees from engaging in prayer or religious activities, whether before, during, or after school hours!*

This incredible court order broadly defined prayer, school events, and school officials in such a way that *employees who bow their heads or fold their hands, pray over meals during their lunch, or merely voice agreement with another's religious discussion at any time on school property or at any school event can be found in contempt of court!*

Principal Frank Lay and Athletic Director Robert Freeman could have lost their retirement benefits if convicted of charges trumped up by the ACLU's activism.

Having worked in the public schools for nearly 30 years, Principal Lay was scheduled to retire the following year from the Santa Rosa County School District. Freeman had given 40 years of his life to public education. Both received a letter from the State of Florida about the criminal contempt charges they were facing. A criminal conviction of a state employee can result in forfeiting accrued retirement benefits.

How could it be in our nation that these dedicated public servants were in jeopardy of paying up to $5,000 in fines and spending six months in prison — not to mention losing pensions earned over the span of their education careers and service to their community — for saying a prayer over a meal?

As I mentioned in this book's Introduction, this travesty began with the ACLU's 2008 national fundraising campaign to raise over 335 million dollars in order to expand its malignant influence across the country. Shortly after announcing it had reached its goal, the ACLU stepped up its activity in several targeted states — Florida being one of them. The ACLU then filed suit against the Santa Rosa School District, located in the Florida Panhandle.

Nine days after a court-ordered decree banning school employees from engaging in or encouraging religious activity (even off campus), Lay and Freeman attended a luncheon to honor private members of the Boosters Club who raised money to build a new athletic field house. The event was attended by adults, not students. Not for a moment did Principal Lay think that merely asking his athletic director to bless the meal would result in criminal charges. But the ACLU complained, and both men were charged with criminal contempt of court.

I cannot fathom the fact that a combined 70 years of dedicated service could be dishonored and tarnished if they were convicted for a single prayer over a meal. These men didn't molest or beat a student. They didn't steal, commit fraud, or harm anyone. One invited the other to offer thanks for a meal, and the other offered a brief prayer of thanksgiving. That's it! No other "crime" was contained in the complaint.

How can something like this happen in America? Indeed, it can happen if the ACLU has its way! We have no intention of letting the ACLU criminalize prayer while making pornography and pedophilia legal.

This is totally outrageous! It is hard to believe this is happening in America.

This is not the America the Founders knew. The Northwest Ordinance of 1787 *required* Territories to teach religion (translated "Christianity") and morality to children in the schools. Today, school officials are being threatened with jail for merely being associated with prayer!

Liberty Counsel could not allow Frank, Michelle, or any other faculty, staff, or student in Santa Rosa County to be thrown in jail for praying! And we could not allow the ACLU to bully them into surrendering their unalienable, God-given rights.

When the ACLU tried to dampen the graduation at Pace High School by forcing the president of the Student Government Association to be removed from the agenda — solely because she is a Christian and might publically express her faith — the students rebelled and rose in unison to recite the Lord's Prayer. Many of them taped crosses to the tops of their graduation caps to demonstrate their Christian faith and to protest this blatant censorship.

Then, Liberty Counsel entered the ring. We went to court to defend Frank, Robert, and Michelle. In addition to representing these school employees, we also filed an intervention on behalf of Christian Educators Association International to represent all of the Christian teachers and staff in the district.

*We wanted to get this oppressive order reversed and bring liberty back to Santa Rosa County.* And like a boxer who has been pressed into a corner, we came out swinging!

## Clear and Present Danger

As I mentioned earlier, on National Constitution Day, 2009, I was in a Florida courtroom for twelve hours defending Santa Rosa County, Florida, Pace High School Principal Frank Lay, and Athletic Director Robert Freeman. As I have related, they were charged with criminal contempt over the simple blessing of a meal. These honorable men faced up to $5,000 in fines, six months in jail, and loss of their collective 70 years of retirement benefits. But by God's grace, Liberty Counsel's litigation team was able to prevail and get the outrageous charges against our clients thrown out. That's when the battle to get the underlying Consent Order declared unconstitutional began!

That's why September 17, 2009, is a day I will never forget. I was profoundly moved by the sights and sounds I experienced. The events of that day made me realize more than ever that we face a "clear and present danger" to our liberty from the ACLU and its atheistic allies.

The early morning began with a driving rain. The downpour briefly stopped as we reached the courthouse. Already, hundreds of people were jammed into the park in front of the building and more lined the adjacent streets.

The rain had not dampened their spirits in the least! Shouts of support and encouragement rang out as we walked past the crowd. The cars crammed together in the parking lots honked their horns and people cheered. Large groups of energetic young people from Pace High School and elsewhere, who had taken the day off from school, expressed their support for Frank and Robert, shouting out that they loved them and were praying for them.

Making our way past security to the fourth floor, I looked down on the crowd. The rain returned, but they didn't seem to care. Their voices rose to the top floor of the courthouse for everyone inside to hear. I turned to walk into the courtroom to prepare for the long day ahead.

In the same courtroom where Frank and Robert were tried as criminals, there hung on the wall a very large picture of our nation's Founding Fathers signing the Constitution. As I fixed my gaze on the picture, my mind raced through the stories of each of these Founders that David Barton, President of Wall-Builders Ministries and one of America's leading historians, had recounted to an assembly of Liberty University School of Law students only three days earlier.

David shared with our law students that on June 28, 1787, just a few weeks before the signing of our Constitution, the Constitutional Convention had begun to unravel. Recognizing the possibility of the convention's failure, Benjamin Franklin rose and delivered his famous speech to remind his bickering colleagues that unless God is the foundation and builder of the house, those who labor to build it do so in vain. He urged the members to pray, and after a three-day prayer meeting at a nearby church, they returned to the same room and our Constitution was born.

*We live in the land of liberty because America was founded upon prayer! Prayer was the turning point in the history of America.* The irony and historical significance of the day's courtroom activities in Pensacola, Florida, were obvious.

After the court was called to order with the prayer, "God save the United States and this Honorable Court," the testimony began. I found it exceedingly odd that the court's crier invoked God, and yet Frank Lay and Robert Freeman were being tried as criminals for doing the same thing!

As one person after another testified, I watched the prosecutor stand before the court and repeatedly turn to look directly at Mr. Lay and Mr. Freeman, who were seated beside me. His voice soared as he told the court and the witnesses in a theatrical and histrionic manner that what these men did was wrong — that the blessing of a meal was the act of a criminal!

*This case in Santa Rosa County, Florida, has made clear once and for all that a key part of the ACLU's radical agenda is nothing less than to criminalize Christianity!*

On that rainy Constitution Day in a federal courtroom, the time finally came when we called our last witness and rested our case. After the closing argument, the judge retreated to her chambers for about 40 minutes, and, of course, her verdict was "Not guilty!"

A wave of relief swept over Frank Lay, Robert Freeman, and their wives, all of whom had been forced to endure a long and torturous ordeal at the hands of the ACLU.

Outside, when the throngs of people heard the decision, tears of joy and shouts of triumph erupted. A representative mixture of people, young and old, of all races and economic backgrounds, had stood outside all day long with signs and umbrellas. Many students who missed class wore bright yellow T-shirts that read, "Lay's Supportive Patriots." Chants of "We came to pray for Lay," the Lord's Prayer, and the singing of familiar hymns could be heard several blocks away from the federal courthouse in Pensacola. The local newspaper reported that the scene resembled a revival.

Upon reflection, the obvious good news is that we won and our clients were free. But the disturbingly bad news is that Liberty Counsel was actually in court fighting against criminal charges over prayer for a meal!

Please don't misunderstand...we all joined the Lays and Freemans in their joyous moment of acquittal. But I was then, and still remain, deeply angered that we had to be there defending honorable, God-fearing public servants who were being treated like criminals for praying.

The day prior to the trial, Congressman Randy Forbes (R-VA), who chairs the Congressional Prayer Caucus, along with more than 60 Members of Congress, wrote Frank and Robert a letter of support. In his public statement, Forbes said this:

> Today it is the school employees in Santa Rosa County. Tomorrow it could be your kid's high school coach, your school's athletic sponsors, or your spouse. If we do not stand up today for our liberties and the right

of all Americans to pray according to their faith, our children and grandchildren will have no foundation left on which to pray.

Congressman Forbes is right. This was a dramatic wake-up call for the people of Florida and the rest of America. Make no mistake: This case will forever be the symbol of the ACLU and its atheistic allies' true agenda — to criminalize Christianity.

I was reminded in Pensacola that Liberty Counsel is quite skillful in defending our liberties when they are attacked. We will likely beat the ACLU every time in a case like this one. But these perilous times demand that we do more than merely defend. Rather, we must aggressively push back and take back the ground. We must "Take Back America!"

Make no mistake: The ACLU is out to destroy America. In addition to their annual budget of about 100 million dollars, the ACLU raised 325 million dollars in 2008-2009 to increase its presence in key "battleground" states. The Santa Rosa County case is just one example of this new aggressiveness. Liberty Counsel must be just as committed to advancing life, liberty, and family as the ACLU is committed to destroying them.

We have an impressive record of victory over the ACLU. If we show up, we can win. But if we don't show up, then people like Frank and Michelle are left alone to fend off criminal contempt charges and jail time against a well-funded foe.

We believe in a different America than does the ACLU. We defended Principal Frank Lay, Athletic Director Robert Freeman and Administrative Assistant Michelle Winkler, and by God's grace, we have won — so far, at least.

We went on the offensive to get the underlying court order the ACLU instigated thrown out. It was this manipulative tactic that gave rise to the charges against our clients in the first place, and it had the potential to ensnare other hapless school district employees if it wasn't totally discredited. In preparing for a subsequent hearing on this case, we learned that the day after Constitution Day (the day we successfully defended Frank and Robert at the federal courthouse in Pensacola), the ACLU sent a letter to the school district, again seeking information that could get Frank Lay thrown into jail.

The ACLU inquired as to why so many people showed up outside the court to pray. "Did Frank Lay have anything to do with this?" they asked. "And why did the students wear T-shirts expressing their support for Principal Lay?" they demanded. "Did Frank have anything to do with causing this behavior?"

The ACLU even asked, "Why did the churches in the community pray for the trial?" "Did Frank Lay encourage the churches to pray?" The ACLU demanded to know if Frank Lay had anything to do with any of these private actions, including private church activities. If he did, they wanted him to be tried as a criminal once again!

Make no mistake: The ACLU wants to criminalize Christianity. That vision is a far different vision than the one we have for America.

I have resolved more than ever to advance our liberties and rebuild the foundations upon which America was built. Through the ministry of Liberty Counsel's litigation arm, we are winning in the nation's courtrooms. Through our office in Washington, DC, the Liberty Center for Law and Policy, and Liberty Counsel Action, we have become a strong voice for truth in the nation's Capital. Through Liberty University School of Law, we are training a new generation of Champions for Christ, who will secure the blessings of liberty for generations to come. And through a growing collaboration of like-minded ministries, Freedom Federation, we are mobilizing a movement.

As I have often said, to win such cases we must show up. To show up, we need you to stand with us! The future of American freedom is literally at stake! We all know that liberty is not free. It is not transmitted in our DNA by the accident of being born in a free society. Liberty requires vigilance. *Every generation of Americans must yearn for liberty and fight to preserve it!*

The ACLU and its allies present a clear and present danger to our liberties. That language has a very specific meaning in our Constitution, and it authorizes the nation to take up arms against an enemy. Together, we must preserve our unalienable right to get down on our knees to pray…but we must never fail to rise up to fight when that freedom is threatened!

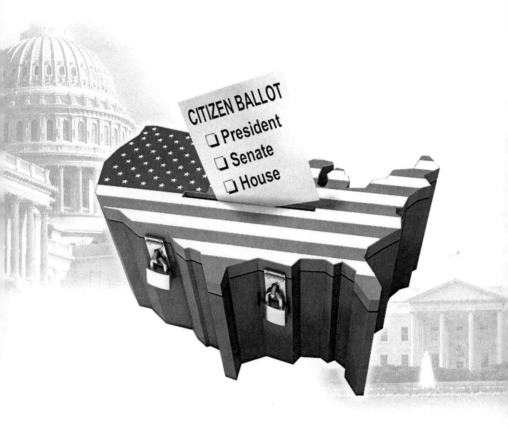

# CHAPTER 2
## God is the Foundation of Government

God is the foundation of good government and national prosperity. Regardless of your religious belief or disbelief, any reasonable person must concede that America is broken. Violent crime plagues not only our inner cities but also our public schools. Even the secular talk show hosts acknowledge that all is not well with America. Something must be done.

Some have postulated that we need more federal money to put extra police officers on the streets and metal detectors in the schools. Some say more guidance counselors addressing violence or laws prohibiting hate speech will remedy the violence. Others argue that we need prayer in our public schools. The answer you reach will, in part, be influenced by the history you know.

America doesn't need another program. Money won't fix our problems. Articulate politicians will not save us. We need God in America again. There is a clear biblical and historical basis for this proposition.

## Biblical Basis

When the nation of Israel was on the verge of entering the Promised Land, Moses knew their future hung in a delicate balance. In order to prepare his people to take the land, he instructed them in the laws of God. The book of Deuteronomy is essentially the second giving of the law or a rehearsing of the law. Except for a few people, those entering the Promised Land were not part of the exodus from Egypt. These people were not around when God gave the Ten Commandments to Moses. Moses, therefore, instructed this young nation in the laws of God.

In Chapter 28 of the book of Deuteronomy, God gives the children of Israel a choice. This is the chapter of the Blessings and the Curses. The choice is clear. The nation can choose to obey God and reap His blessings, or disobey God and incur the inevitable curses. There are two paths to choose. The first path is outlined in verses 1-14 and the second path is revealed in verses 15-68. The only difference in following one path as opposed to the other is how the nation corporately, and people individually, relate to God. If you accept God and follow His commands, then you will inevitably be blessed. On the contrary, if you reject God and His laws, you will reap the inevitable result of your choice.

When you purchase a car, you have a series of choices to make. You can follow the owner's manual to prolong the life of the car, or you can ignore the manufacturer's warnings and reap the consequences. If you drive your car without oil, the engine will inevitably blow. The manufacturer didn't cause the engine to blow. You did. The manufacturer gave you guidance on how to properly maintain the car. It is up to you to follow these rules or reject them. It is the same with the teachings of Deuteronomy. God simply reminds us of the inevitable result of our choice to reject Him.

The blessings portion of Deuteronomy 28 begins in verse 1.

If you fully obey the Lord your God and carefully follow
all His commands I give you today, the Lord your God
will set you high above all the nations on earth.

If you obey God and follow His commands, then verse 3 says you will be blessed in the city. Verse 6 says, "You will be blessed when you come in and blessed when you go out." This verse pictures a city free of violence. The doors of the walled city are not shut. They remain open. There is no reason to shut them because there is no violence in or outside the city. You will be as safe and secure in the city as you will be when you travel outside the city.

Verses 4-5 say that you will be blessed in your gross national product. The production of goods, services, and food will be plentiful. Verse 4 indicates that both animal and human reproduction will continue to be at peak levels.

The fruit of your womb will be blessed, and the crops of
your land and the young of your livestock — calves of
your herds and the lambs of your flocks. Your basket and
your kneading trough will be blessed.

Another consequence of following God and His commandments is that you will experience peace and security. You will not only have domestic security as indicated in verse 6, but you will have international security as outlined in verse 7. Chapter 28, verse 7, indicates that whenever an enemy will attack, the enemy will come in one way, but be forced to flee in multiple directions. The military might will be unsurpassable by enemy nations.

> The Lord will grant that the enemies who rise up against you will be defeated before you. They will come at you from one direction, but flee from you in seven.

One of the blessings that flows from obeying God is abundant prosperity. Other people on earth will know that you serve the Lord. Corporately you will lend to many nations and not borrow. God finished instructing Moses regarding the blessings in verses 9-14:

> The Lord will establish you as His holy people, as He promised you on oath, if you keep the commands of the Lord your God and walk in His ways. Then all the peoples on earth will see that you are called by the name of the Lord, and they will fear you. The Lord will grant you abundant prosperity — in the fruit of your womb, the young of your livestock and the crops of your ground — in the land he swore to your forefathers to give you. The Lord will open the heavens, the storehouse of His bounty, to send rain on your land in season and to bless all the work of your hands. You will lend to many nations but will borrow from none. The Lord will make you the head, not the tail. If you pay attention to the commands of the Lord your God that I give you this day and carefully follow them, you will always be at the top,

never at the bottom. Do not turn aside from any of His commands I give you today, to the right or to the left, following other gods and serving them.

However, Deuteronomy 28, verse 15, begins the curses. Verse 15 states that if you do not obey God, all of the curses will hunt you down and devour you corporately and individually.

If you disobey God, you will be cursed in your city. Verse 16 pictures a city in shambles, both morally and economically. In America today, we have cities which are bankrupt. One of the leading centers for murder is our nation's capital in Washington, DC. Many cities no longer have sufficient funds to adequately staff their police forces. Many city streets are now lined with potholes.

Verses 17-18 say you will be cursed in your field. The production of goods and services will lag behind international competitors. Today many agricultural producers are on the verge of collapse. We face a crisis in America because of the rising cost of labor and the decreased amount of exports.

In verse 18, Deuteronomy states that a disobedient nation will experience infertility in both animals and humans. Today, millions of children have been slaughtered by abortion. Thousands of women have become sterile.

Chapter 28, verse 19, states that we will no longer have security if we reject God. I remember growing up as a little boy in a rural Florida town. We lived in a trailer without air conditioning. During the day we would leave the trailer door wide open. Never did we fear that an intruder would break into our home. When we went shopping at the local mall, we kept the windows down in our car and did not lock the doors. I remember many people leaving keys in their car. It was unheard of to have your car stolen. However, today we lock the doors during the day, even though we are home. We install burglar alarms to guard our dwelling while we are absent and during the night. Hardly anyone leaves their car doors unlocked when they park the car in public. We even lock our car doors during the day when the car is parked in our driveway.

Verse 20 states that we will experience confusion if we reject God. Certainly we are confused today when we have to debate the most elementary topic of marriage. It should be obvious that marriage is confined to a lasting relationship between a man and a woman. However, when we have to debate today about same-sex marriage, we have digressed in our thinking rather than advanced. We are confused in our reasoning.

Today we no longer have a platform from which we can argue our differences. There is no longer any common ground. If I have to debate with you that a couch is green rather than red, we will not be able to enter into an intelligent discussion if you don't even acknowledge that the couch exists. That is the state of affairs today.

Verses 21, 27-28 and 60-61 paint a startling picture regarding incurable diseases.

The Lord will plague you with diseases until He has destroyed you from the land you are entering to possess.

*  *  *

The Lord will afflict you with the boils of Egypt and with tumors, festering sores and the itch, from which you cannot be cured. The Lord will afflict you with madness, blindness and confusion of mind.

\* \* \*

He will bring upon you all the diseases of Egypt that you dreaded, and they will cling to you. The Lord will also bring on you every kind of sickness and disaster not recorded in this Book of the Law, until you are destroyed.

In the context of Deuteronomy 28, verses 27-28 refer to the incurable diseases of Egypt. We know historically that the Egyptians were plagued with incurable sexually transmitted diseases. Today, we have several incurable STDs, not the least of which are HPV and HIV/AIDS. Today we not only have incurable diseases, we have new diseases which we have never encountered. We do not know their origin, let alone their cause or cure.

When I was pastoring, a doctor in my church who went to medical school in the 1960s stated that it was unheard of to think of a new disease. He was taught that we knew all the diseases. We just didn't know all the cures. Today, we are clueless as to the cures for many diseases. We have new diseases arising all the time. Existing diseases change forms. Creating antibodies has become a continuing challenge. We have new diseases unrelated to the previous ones we've encountered. We are on the verge of a viral epidemic in this country based upon our overuse of antibiotics. Incurable diseases are a natural consequence of rejecting God.

Verse 30 speaks of infidelity. It describes a situation where a man marries a woman, but another man sleeps with her. Statistics that say divorce has leveled off or slightly decreased are inaccurate, because fewer people are getting married. More people are choosing to live together without getting married.

Another consequence of disobeying God is a weak military. Verse 36 depicts an army with weak leadership. A foreign king will lead this army. Today, we are so wrapped up in a one world order concept under the leadership of the United Nations that we have forgotten our military dominance and our fierce independence.

A nation that rejects God will be a debtor nation. Verse 44 indicates that a nation rejecting God will be a debtor rather than a lender to its international neighbors. Today, we are the biggest debtor nation on earth. Our nation not only is in debt to other nations, our people are also burdened with debt. Quick financing with the allure of accumulating things has strapped our spendable income. Debt crushes America and breaks up families.

Deuteronomy 28, verses 56-57, illustrate the epitome of rejecting God:

> The most gentle and sensitive woman among you — so sensitive and gentle that she would not venture to touch the ground with the sole of her foot — will begrudge the husband she loves and her own son or daughter, the afterbirth from her womb and the children she bears. For she intends to eat them secretly during the siege and in the distress that your enemy will inflict on you and your cities.

Verse 56 pictures a delicate woman who is so tender that she can't even put her bare foot on the ground. This delicate picture of femininity will turn against her husband and hate him. She will also turn against her children and kill them.

In context, the circumstance causing her to kill her children is famine. Then it was famine, today it's convenience. The woman who is supposed to be the protector of her child is now its destroyer. The womb is the most dangerous place for a child. Abortion has now morphed into infanticide with late-term abortion. Euthanasia has already gripped part of the country with Oregon being the first state to officially legalize euthanasia.

The lessons of Deuteronomy 28 are clear. God has given us a choice. There are two paths we can follow. If we accept God and obey His commands, then the blessings of verses 1-14 are the inevitable result. However, if we reject God and do not follow His commandments, then verses 15-68 describe our ultimate demise. Deuteronomy clearly outlines the biblical basis for the proposition that God is the foundation for good government and national prosperity.

## Historical Basis

Deuteronomy Chapter 28 clearly outlines the proposition that God is the foundation of good government. Our early documents penned by our founding fathers also outline the historical basis for this same proposition. In 1776, the Declaration of Independence marked the beginning of our country's independence. Thomas Jefferson indicated that the Declaration of Independence was "an expression of the American mind."[1]  In relevant part, the Declaration states as follows:

> When in the course of human events, it becomes necessary for one people to dissolve the political bands which have connected them with another, and to assume among the Powers of the earth, the separate and equal station to which the Laws of Nature and of Nature's God entitle them, a decent respect to the opinions of mankind requires that they should declare the causes which impel them to the separation.

> We hold these truths to be self-evident, that all men are created equal, that they are endowed by their Creator with certain unalienable Rights that among these are Life, Liberty, and the pursuit of Happiness.

> That to secure these rights, Governments are instituted among Men, deriving their just powers from the consent of the governed.

> That whenever any Form of Government becomes destructive of these ends, it is the Right of the People to alter or to abolish it, to institute new Government, laying its foundation on such principles and organizing its powers in such form, as to them shall seem most likely to affect their Safety and Happiness…. But when a long train of abuses and usurpations, pursuing invariably the same Object, evinces a design to reduce them under absolute Despotism, it is their right, it is their duty, to

throw off such Government, and to provide new Guards for their future security....

The first paragraph of the Declaration states that when in the course of human history it becomes necessary for a once unified people to dissolve their government, it is necessary to document the reasons which impel them to the separation. It was a bold step for our founding fathers to separate from their homeland in order to create a separate government with equal power and standing on earth. The founders wanted to make clear the reasons that caused this drastic step.

The second paragraph of the Declaration states the central proposition: "We hold these truths to be self-evident..." These truths are not debatable. They are self-evident. These truths predate government. No government can add to or take away from these truths. These truths cannot be modified. These truths are not up for vote or debate. They are self-evident and God-given. What are these truths?

These self-evident truths are that all men are created equal, they are endowed with certain unalienable rights, that among these are life, liberty, and the pursuit of happiness. The rights delineated are unalienable. Government cannot take them away and government cannot give them. The Supreme Court has no jurisdiction to nullify these rights. In other words, the Supreme Court and the other branches of government must protect these rights.

The Declaration answers the question: What is government and why do we need government? Whenever we come together to form a social relationship, we create rules to govern our interaction. It doesn't matter what title we give these rules. The rules we make we call "government." Whether it is a republic, a democracy, an oligarchy, a monarchy, or communism, it is still called "government." We assign tasks to one another and we outline our various rights and duties. The Declaration indicates that in order "to secure these rights, governments are instituted among men, deriving their just powers from the consent of the governed."

The sole purpose of government is to secure "these rights," namely the rights to equal opportunity, to life, liberty, and the pursuit of happiness. That is the purpose of government. When viewed properly, the historical basis for government is to secure certain God-given, unalienable rights. The role of government is, therefore, limited. Government is to be a protector of God-given rights, not an enemy of them.

However, "whenever any form of government becomes destructive of these ends, it is the right of the people to alter or to abolish it...." It is, therefore, the right of the people "to institute new government, laying its foundation on such principles and organizing its powers in such form, as to them shall seem most likely to affect their Safety and Happiness." When government persists in a pattern of abuses which inevitably pursue the same object to reduce the governed under absolute despotism, then "it is their right, it is their duty, to throw off such government, and to provide new guards for their future security...." The Declaration is clear that rebellion against government should not occur for a simple mistake or an occasional misstep. But, when government, whatever its form, sets a course to no longer protect these God-given, unalienable rights, it is not only our right, it is our "duty" to alter, or if necessary, to abolish it. This is the point in history at which the colonists found themselves. The American Revolution must not be considered a one-time past event. Revolution may be necessary at any given point in history whenever government no longer protects our God-given, unalienable rights.

The purpose of government is to preserve life, liberty, and the pursuit of happiness. There is no question that our early founders presupposed our country was to be based upon Jesus Christ and Judeo-Christian principles of morality and virtue.

The first Colonial grant from Queen Elizabeth to Sir Walter Raleigh in 1584 was stipulated for the purpose to enact laws provided "they be not against the true Christian faith."[2]  In other words, the monetary grant used to form this new colony had a stipulation — no law should be enacted under this grant that would in any way be contrary to the true Christian faith.

The United States Supreme Court in 1872, in the case of *The Church of the Holy Trinity*, stated on three separate occasions that "this is a Christian nation," "we are a Christian people," and "this is a Christian nation."[3]

George Washington, our first general and first President of the United States, stated, "Reason and experience both forbid us to expect that national morality can prevail in the exclusion of religious principle."[4]

John Quincy Adams, the sixth United States President, stated that the "highest glory of the American Revolution was this: it connected in one indissoluble bond, the principles of civil government with the principles of Christianity."[5]  Can you imagine if today's politicians would echo the words of John Quincy Adams? The liberal media would crucify them.

John Adams, our first Vice President and second President, hit the nail on the head when he stated:

> We have no government armed with power capable of contending with human passions unbridled by morality and religion. Avarice, ambition, revenge, or gallantry, would break the strongest cords of our Constitution as a whale goes through a net. Our Constitution was made only for a moral and religious people. It is wholly inadequate to the government of any other.[6]

The founders presupposed that we, the governed, would have self-restraint. Unbridled human passion results in destruction and chaos. Our passions must be restrained. These passions will be restrained either internally or externally. The founders presupposed that our passions would be self-restrained. We have an internal restraint based upon Jesus Christ and Judeo-Christian morality and virtue. In the absence of this self-restraint, the only other alternative is external restraint. If we are not self-restrained, then the government must restrain us.

Our constitutional republic was designed as a limited form of government with very little external restraints on the people. Few restraints were necessary because the founders presupposed self-restraint. If we are not self-restrained, then the liberties acknowledged and protected by our Constitution will result in chaos. That is why it is so easy in this country for a terrorist to cause destruction.

For example, if parents do not restrain their children from being downtown after midnight during the week, then government will by enacting curfew laws. Government will take away our external liberties to the extent that our internal passion is unrestrained. No form of government, republic or dictatorship, can restrain an unrestrained people.

On July 21, 1789, the First Continental Congress adopted the Northwest Ordinance that was originally drafted by Thomas Jefferson and enacted by Congress under the Articles of Confederation on July 13, 1787. The Ordinance states: "Religion, morality and knowledge, being necessary to good government and the happiness of mankind, schools and the means of education shall be forever encouraged."[7]  Since religion and morality were necessary to good government, the means of inculcating these values were through public and private schools. There was no thought of "separation of church and state" between religion and the public schools at the time of the First Continental Congress. Indeed, public schools were considered the vehicle through which religion and morality would be taught to our new generation.

Dr. Benjamin Rush, one of the signers of the Declaration, stated the following in *A Defense of the Use of the Bible in Schools*:

> The only means of establishing and perpetrating our republican forms of government...is the universal education of our youth in the principles of Christianity by the means of the Bible.[8]

The first compulsory school law was entitled, "The Old Deluder Satan Act." Drafted in 1647, the law stated that because "one chief project of that old deluder, Satan, [is] to keep men from the knowledge of the Scriptures," public schools were necessary to teach people to read.[9]

Harvard was the first college in America. Founded in 1636, the official Harvard motto was, "For Christ and the Church."[10] Harvard, Princeton, Yale, William and Mary, Rutgers, and Columbia are just a few of the well-known universities that had Christian origins. Of the one hundred twenty-six original colleges in America, one hundred twenty-three were based on Christian principles.[11]

Benjamin Harris's school textbook, *The New England Primer*, was one of the most influential school textbooks in the history of American education. It was first printed in 1690 and was continually used from then until 1900, a span of two hundred and ten years. In a 1777 edition, the first section contained the rhyming alphabet. A partial example includes the following:

A — In Adam's fall we sinned all.

C — Christ crucify'd for sinners dy'd.

D — The deluge drown'd the Earth around.

\* \* \*

H — My book and heart must never part.

\* \* \*

Z — Zaccheus did climb the tree our Lord to see.

In another section, *The New England Primer* contained the alphabet with Bible verses:

E. Except a man be born again he cannot
   see the kingdom of God.

* * *

L. Liars shall have their part in the lake which
   burns with fire and brimstone.

* * *

N. Now is the accepted time, now is the day of Salvation.

Since there were no grade levels at the time of our founding fathers, the following test would be equivalent to the first grade. See how well you score.

What offices does Christ execute as our Redeemer?

How does Christ execute the office of a prophet?

How does Christ execute the office of a priest?

How does Christ execute the office of a king?

Which is the fifth commandment?

What is required in the fifth commandment?

What is forbidden in the fifth commandment?

What is the reason annexed in the fifth commandment?

Bonus question — What are the benefits which in this life do accompany or flow from justification, adoption and sanctification?

Remember the above test was universally distributed in all schools. Today, how would our public school students score on this test? Would our Sunday school students pass this test? How well did you score?[12]

Noah Webster graduated from Yale University. He was an expert in grammar and mastered twenty-eight languages. Although he authored many school textbooks, his most famous one was produced in 1828, known as the *American Dictionary of the English Language*. In less than two decades, approximately twenty-four million copies of his dictionaries were sold. Noah Webster was a devout Christian, as evidenced by his personal testimony contained in the 1854 edition of the dictionary. Noah Webster believed that Christianity was central to education and government:

> The Christian religion is the most important and one of the first things in which all children under a free government, ought to be instructed…No truth is more evident to my mind than that the Christian religion must be the basis of any government intended to secure the rights and privileges of a free people.[13]

If anyone doubts the effectiveness of this country's early education, try spelling the following words: loquacious, sagacious, mucilaginous, legerdemain, duodecimo, imperceptibility, perpendicularity, and incomprehensibility. These words were required spelling for what we would classify today as elementary students.

There is a clear biblical and historical basis for the proposition that God is the foundation of good government and national prosperity. This proposition is presupposed in Deuteronomy

Chapter 28. It is also presupposed in America's founding documents. The Declaration of Independence is probably the best historical document that outlines the purpose and place of government and religion. Government's role is to protect and preserve certain God-given, unalienable, self-evident rights. Government will self-destruct if the governed are no longer self-restrained by morality and virtue. Government must be changed, or if necessary abolished, if it no longer protects these liberties.

# CHAPTER 3
## Our Country Has Displaced God
## As Our Foundation

Today our country has displaced God as our foundation and replaced Him with human reason. The result is uncontrolled human passion, which will inevitably lead to self-destruction.

### Separation of Church and State

This country was established upon the assumption that religion was essential to good government. On July 13, 1787, the Continental Congress enacted the Northwest Ordinance, which stated: "Religion, morality and knowledge, being necessary to good government and the happiness of mankind, schools and the means of education shall be forever encouraged."[1] The First Amendment prohibited the federal government from establishing a religion to which the several states must pay homage. The First Amendment provided assurance that the federal government would not meddle in the affairs of religion within the sovereign states.

Today, groups like the American Civil Liberties Union and Americans United for Separation of Church and State have attempted to create an environment wherein government and religion are adversaries. Their favorite phrase has been "separation of church and state." These groups have intoned the mantra of "separation of church and state" so long that many people believe the phrase is in the Constitution. In Proverbs Chapter 18, verse 16, the Bible says, "He who states his case first seems right until another comes to challenge him." I'm sure you have seen legal arguments on television where the prosecution argues to the jury that the defendant is guilty. Once the prosecution finishes the opening presentation, you believe that the defendant is guilty. However, after the defense attorney completes the rebuttal presentation of the argument, you may be confused, or at least you acknowledge that the case is not clear-cut.

The same is true with the phrase "separation of church and state." The ACLU and the liberal media have touted the phrase so many times that most people believe the phrase is in the Constitution. Nowhere is "separation of church and state" referenced in the Constitution. This phrase was in the former Soviet Union's Constitution, but it has never been part of the United States Constitution.

Justice Oliver Wendell Holmes once said, "It is one of the misfortunes of the law that ideas become encysted in phrases, and thereafter for a long time cease to provoke further analysis."[2] The phrase, "separation of church and state," has become one of these misfortunes of law.

In 1947 the Supreme Court popularized Thomas Jefferson's phrase "wall of separation between church and state."[3] Taking the Jefferson metaphor out of context, strict separationists have often used the phrase to silence Christians and to limit any Christian influence from affecting the political system. To understand Jefferson's "wall of separation," we should return to the original context in which it was written. Jefferson himself once wrote:

> On every question of construction, [we must] carry ourselves back to the time when the constitution was adopted, recollect the spirit manifested in the debates, and instead of trying what meaning may be squeezed out of the test, or invented against it, conform to the probable one in which it was a part.[4]

Thomas Jefferson was inaugurated as the third President on March 4, 1801. On October 7, 1801, a committee of the Danbury Baptist Association wrote a congratulatory letter to Jefferson on his election as President. Organized in 1790, the Danbury Baptist Association was an alliance of churches in Western Connecticut. The Baptists were a religious minority in the state of Connecticut where Congregationalism was the established church.[5]

The concern of the Danbury Baptist Association is understandable once we consider the background of church-state relations in Great Britain. The Association eschewed the kind of state-sponsored enforcement of religion that had been the norm in Great Britain.

The Danbury Baptist Association committee wrote to the President stating, "Religion is at all times and places a Matter between God and Individuals — that no man ought to suffer in Name, person or affects on account of his religious Opinions."[6]

The Danbury Baptists believed that religion was an unalienable right and they hoped that Jefferson would raise the consciousness of the people to recognize religious freedom as unalienable. However, the Danbury Baptists acknowledged that the President of the United States was not a "national Legislator," and they also understood that the "national government cannot destroy the Laws of each State."[7] In other words, they recognized Jefferson's limited influence as the federal executive on the individual states.

Jefferson did not necessarily like receiving mail as President, but he generally endeavored to turn his responses into an opportunity to sow what he called "useful truths" and principles among the people so that the ideas might take political root. He, therefore, took this opportunity to explain why he as President, contrary to his predecessors, did not proclaim national days of fasting and prayer.

Jefferson's letter went through at least two drafts. Part of the first draft reads as follows:

> Believing with you that religion is a matter which lies solely between man and his god, that he owes account to none other for his faith or his worship, that legitimate powers of government reach actions only and not opinions, I contemplate with sovereign reverence that act of the whole American people which declared that their legislature should make no law respecting an establishment of religion, or prohibiting the free exercise thereof; thus building a wall of separation between church and state. Congress thus inhibited from acts respecting reli-

gion, and the Executive authorized only to execute their acts, I have refrained from prescribing even occasional performances of devotion....[8]

Jefferson asked Levi Lincoln, the Attorney General, and Gideon Granger, the Postmaster General, to comment on his draft. In a letter to Mr. Lincoln, Jefferson stated he wanted to take the occasion to explain why he did not "proclaim national fastings and thanksgivings, as my predecessors did."[9] He knew that the response would "give great offense to the New England clergy" and he advised Lincoln that he should suggest necessary changes.[10]

Mr. Lincoln responded that the five New England states have always been in the habit of "observing fasts and thanksgivings in performance of proclamations from the respective Executives" and that this "custom is venerable being handed down from our ancestors."[11] Lincoln, therefore, struck through the last sentence of the above quoted letter about Jefferson refraining from prescribing even occasional performances of devotion. Jefferson penned a note in the margin that this paragraph was omitted because "it might give uneasiness to some of our republican friends in the eastern states where the proclamation of thanksgivings" by their state executives is respected.[12]

To understand Jefferson's use of the wall metaphor in his letter to the Danbury Baptist Association, we must compare his other writings. On March 4, 1805, in Jefferson's Second Inaugural Address, he stated as follows:

In matters of religion, I have considered that its free exercise is placed by the Constitution independent of the powers of the General [i.e., federal] Government. I have, therefore, undertaken, on no occasion, to prescribe the religious exercises suited to it; but have left them, as the Constitution found them, under the direction and discipline of State or Church authorities acknowledged by the several religious societies.[13]

Then on January 23, 1808, Jefferson wrote in response to a letter received by Reverend Samuel Miller, who requested him to declare a national day of thanksgiving and prayer:

I consider the government of the United States as interdicted by the Constitution from intermeddling with religious institutions, their doctrines, discipline, or exercises. This results not only from the provisions that no law shall be made respecting the establishment or free exercise of religion [First Amendment], but from that also which reserves to the States the powers not delegated to the United States [Tenth Amendment]. Certainly no power to prescribe any religious exercise, or to assume authority in religious discipline, has been delegated to the General [i.e., federal] Government. It must then rest with the States, as far as it can be in any human authority.[14]

\* \* \*

I am aware that the practice of my predecessors may be quoted. But I have every belief, that the example of State executives led to the assumption of that authority by the General Government, without due examination, which would have discovered that what might be a right in State government, was a violation of that right when assumed by another.... [C]ivil powers alone have been given to the President of the United States, and no authority to direct the religious exercises of his constituents.[15]

Comparing these two responses to his actions in the state government of Virginia shows the true intent of Jefferson's wall metaphor. As a member of the House of Burgesses, on May 24, 1774, Jefferson participated in drafting and enacting a resolution designating a "Day of Fasting, Humiliation, and Prayer."[16] This resolution occurred only a few days before he wrote "A Bill for Establishing Religious Freedom." In 1779, while Jefferson was governor of Virginia, he issued a proclamation decreeing a day "of publick and solemn thanksgiving and prayer to Almighty God." In the late 1770s, as chair of the Virginia committee of Revisers, Jefferson was the chief architect of a measure entitled, "A Bill for Appointing Days of Public Fasting and Thanksgiving." Interestingly, this bill authorized the Governor or Chief Magistrate with the advice of Counsel, to designate days of thanksgiving and fasting and required that the public be notified by proclamation. The bill also provided that "[e]very minister of the gospel shall on each day so to be appointed, attend and perform divine service and preach a sermon, or discourse, suited to the occasion, in his church, on pain of forfeiting fifty pounds for every failure, not having a reasonable excuse."[17] Although the bill was never enacted, Jefferson was its chief architect, and the sponsor was none other than James Madison.

So what did Jefferson mean when he used the "wall" metaphor? Jefferson undoubtedly meant that the First Amendment prohibited the federal Congress from enacting any law respecting an establishment of religion or prohibiting the free exercise thereof. As the chief executive of the federal government, the President's duty was to carry out the directives of Congress. If Congress had no authority in matters of religion then neither did the President. Religion was clearly within the jurisdiction of the church and states. As a state legislator, Jefferson saw no problem with proclaiming days of thanksgiving and prayer, and even on one occasion prescribed a penalty to the clergy for failure to abide by these state proclamations. Jefferson believed that the Constitution created a limited government and that the states retained the authority over matters of religion not only through the First Amendment, but also through the Tenth Amendment.[18] The federal government had absolutely no jurisdiction over religion, as that matter was left where the Constitution found it, namely with the individual churches and the several states.

In summary, the First Amendment says more about federalism than religious freedom. In other words, the purpose of the First Amendment was to declare that the federal government had absolutely no jurisdiction in matters of religion. It could neither establish a religion nor prohibit the free exercise of religion. The First Amendment clearly erected a barrier between the federal government and religion on a state level. If a state chose to have no religion, or to have an established religion, the federal government had no jurisdiction one way or the other. This is what Thomas Jefferson meant by the "wall of separation." In context, the word "state" really referred to the federal government. The First Amendment did not apply to the states. It was only applicable as a restraint against the federal government. The problem arose in 1940[19] and then again in 1947,[20] when the Supreme Court applied the First Amendment to the states. This turned the First Amendment on its head, and completely inverted its meaning.[21] The First Amendment was never meant to be a restraint on state government. It was only applicable to the federal government. When the Supreme Court turned the First Amendment around 180 degrees and used Jefferson's comment in the process, it not only perverted the First Amendment, but misconstrued the intent of Jefferson's letter.

There is nothing wrong with the way Jefferson used the "wall of separation between church and state" metaphor. The problem has arisen when the Supreme Court in 1947 erroneously picked up the metaphor and attempted to construct a constitutional principle. While the metaphor understood in its proper context is useful, we might do well to heed the words of the United States Supreme Court Justice William Rehnquist:

> The "wall of separation between church and State" is a metaphor based on bad history, a metaphor which has proved useless as a guide to judging. It should be frankly and explicitly abandoned.[22]

Jefferson used the phrase "wall of separation between church and state" as a means of expressing his republican view that the federal or general government should not interfere with religious matters among the several states. In its proper context, the phrase represents a clear expression of state autonomy.

Accordingly, Jefferson saw no contradiction in authoring a religious proclamation to be used by state officials and refusing to issue similar religious proclamations as President of the United States. His wall had less to do with the separation of church and *all* civil government than with the separation of federal and state governments.[23]

The "wall of separation between church and state" phrase, as understood by Jefferson, was never meant to exclude people of faith from influencing and shaping government. Jefferson would be shocked to learn that his letter has been used as a weapon against religion. He would never countenance such shabby and distorted use of history.

## The Supreme Court as Change Agent

The biggest destroyer of American values and religious freedom in this country has been the United States Supreme Court. Although originally the Supreme Court had no jurisdiction over religious matters among the individual states, it nevertheless usurped this authority, and this power grab went unchallenged by the governed. We have allowed the Supreme Court to amass power it was never granted. With its new self-appointed power unchecked by the people, the Supreme Court turned its destructive cannons on religion and public schools in 1962 and 1963. During those years, the Supreme Court ruled school-sponsored prayer and Bible reading unconstitutional. In one case, the Supreme Court quoted an alleged expert's testimony in the trial court where he stated: "If portions of the New Testament were read without explanation, they could be and…had been psychologically harmful to the child…"[24]

In 1980 the Supreme Court realigned its war cannons toward the public schools one more time. This time, the Court stripped the Ten Commandments from a classroom bulletin board in a Kentucky public school. The rationale used by the Supreme Court was that the students might actually view the Ten Commandments as they hung on the classroom bulletin board and be induced to observe their dictates. If this occurred, the Court felt the result would be an unconstitutional establishment of religion.[25] The Supreme Court had the audacity to state the following:

> If the posted copies of the Ten Commandments are to have any effect at all, it will be to induce the school-children to read, meditate upon, perhaps to venerate and obey, the Commandments. However desirable this might be as a matter of private devotion, it is not a permissible state objective under the Establishment Clause.[26]

The Supreme Court was at least right about one thing. Since the Court removed the Ten Commandments, students no longer observe them. Metal detectors have now replaced the Ten Commandments.

The "separation of church and state" mantra intoned by the ACLU has wrought untold damage to America. The following cases are illustrations of situations that we have encountered at Liberty Counsel. While some of these cases may seem bizarre, we have investigated each one and found the facts to be true.

In Duluth, Minnesota, an accountant became blind from diabetes. He required dialysis three times per week. He received this dialysis at a local hospital. While there, he watched religious programming on his private TV. He also occasionally shared his faith in Christ with other interested patients. The head nurse told him that he could no longer watch religious programming on his own TV and he must stop talking about Jesus to other patients. If he did not cease this activity, she threatened to unplug him from the dialysis machine and refuse him further treatment. The facts are so shocking that we thought this man must be disruptive. We interviewed his driver who confirmed the facts. We also spoke to other patients. No other patient had ever complained. The only one who had complained was the head nurse. Her threats to unplug him and refuse treatment were literally death threats engendered solely by his Christian witness.

In West Allis, Wisconsin, Chris Pfeifer founded the Genesis Commission. Chris has not always been a Christian. In fact, at one time he was an agnostic steeped in evolution. After he accepted Christ, he began studying the origins of the universe. He then became convinced of creation.

Chris applied to use a public meeting room in a public library in West Allis. The name of the room was the Constitution Room. The policy provided that anyone could use the room for meetings, but the policy prohibited any religious viewpoint. When Chris handed in his application, he was told that it would probably be denied because of the Christian nature of his meeting. He was also told that he could not have prayer in the Constitution Room. Once the application was denied, Liberty Counsel filed suit. During the depositions, the Library Director acknowledged that any topic can be discussed in the Constitution Room except religion. In fact, at the conclusion of the deposition, I placed various library books on the desk in front of the Director. He acknowledged that these books were from the Library. These books addressed Christianity and creation. He stated that Chris could read these books privately by himself in a library carrel, but he could not walk across the hall to the Constitution Room and tell others about them because that would be religious instruction prohibited by the policy.[27]

In Crown Point, Indiana, the Northwest Community Church and its pastor, Steve Buchelt, sought to rent school facilities for his new church. The church began meeting at the school auditorium on Sunday mornings. However, when the rental contract was presented to the Superintendent for final approval, the Superintendent evicted the church without notice. The policy allowed secular groups to rent the school facilities, but not religious groups.

After Liberty Counsel filed suit, the School Board Attorney was terminated and we were able to resolve the case by drafting a new policy. Several weeks after the church began meeting in the school auditorium, I had the pleasure of preaching at the church. I was surprised to observe a plaque in the auditorium foyer that read, "Freedom Shrine," surrounded by historical documents. One of the documents was The Northwest Ordinance. I pointed out a sentence in the Ordinance to Pastor Buchelt that read, "Religion, morality and education, being necessary to good government and the happiness of mankind, schools and the means of education shall be forever encouraged." Had the school officials and their attorney read and understood these documents, which have been displayed in the auditorium for years, they would have welcomed the church.

In Deland, Florida, a third grade teacher told her students they could select any book to bring to class and read as long as the book did not mention God. In Ithaca, New York, a student was told by her teacher to remove her book cover because it listed the Ten Commandments. The teacher stated that the book cover could not be brought into the public school because of the "separation of church and state." The teacher also told the student that she could no longer wear her gold cross necklace on the outside of her blouse. She was told to tuck the cross under her blouse.

In Orlando, Florida, a six-year-old was asked by his fellow classmate at recess about the meaning of Easter. He told his classmate that it was about God raising Jesus from the dead. When the teacher overheard him, she told him that he could not talk about God in the public schools because of the "separation of church and state."

Jessie was an eleven-year-old special needs child. Jessie's class threw a birthday party for her. Jessie got excited so her mother, who attended the party, took Jessie into the kitchen to pray with her. A teacher's aide and another student overheard Jessie's mother praying and told school officials. The school officials then told Jessie's mother that she could never again pray with her daughter while she was on the school campus.

When Christopher was in the second grade, his teacher asked the class to make a Valentine card as a school project. His card said, "Roses are red. Violets are blue. Did you know that Jesus loves you?" When he handed in his card like the other students, the teacher singled out his card and gave it back. She said that he could not use the word "Jesus" in public school because it violates the "separation of church and state."

In the case of *Adler v. Duval County School Board*,[28] the school has a policy that provides students with an opportunity to present a two-minute message at the beginning and/or conclusion of their graduation. The policy never mentions the word "prayer." The students can have any message, whether it's secular, sacred, profane or profound. The ACLU filed suit, claiming that the students might use the two-minute message for some kind of religious topic or worse — they might even pray. The ACLU argued that if the students said anything religious, this would somehow violate the Constitution. Fortunately, we successfully defended this case brought by the ACLU. However, this case illustrates the absurdity of the ACLU's "separation of church and state" position. In the view of the ACLU, students can say anything they want as long as it is not religious. This position is a far cry from the understanding of our founding fathers.

In Waukesha, Wisconsin, Robert Thompson desired to pass out Bibles and pocket-sized copies of the United States Constitution and the Declaration of Independence in a public park. He was surprised to come across the county park ordinance that stated if anyone wanted to talk about politics or religion with another person in the park, they first needed to receive prior permission from county officials. Also, the policy completely prohibited the distribution of any religious or political material in the public park. Robert thought surely this must be a mistake, so he went to the county office and was told by officials that he could not pass out religious or political literature, and if he didn't like the Ordinance, he could sue them. We did, and we won. The policy has now been redrafted and Robert can pass out his Bibles.

In Marietta, Georgia, Art and Norma Ellison host a Friday evening prayer meeting in their home as part of cell group meetings of their local church. Approximately six to eight people attend the Friday evening meetings. Most of the time, everyone parks in the Ellison's driveway. There is no loud music and no disruption. To their astonishment, Art and Norma received a letter from the Planning and Zoning Commission, stating that the couple was in violation of a zoning code because their house was in a residential district and they were conducting "church" in an unauthorized area. The letter warned that the couple must immediately cease and desist the home prayer meeting. We found out that the city allowed other secular meetings such as Boy Scouts, Girl Scouts, Amway and Mary Kay meetings in local homes. Other people gathered to watch Monday night football. On the eve of filing a lawsuit, I faxed a letter to the city zoning officials demanding that the city retract the letter immediately or otherwise face a federal suit. Fortunately, the city retracted the letter. However, in another case, a couple in Denver, Colorado, had to litigate the issue because there, the city zoning officials stated that the prayer meeting could be conducted in a home one time per month, but anything more than that violates the city zoning laws.

In Syracuse, New York, Antonio Peck attended kindergarten. The teacher told the class to draw a poster reflecting their understanding of the environment. Antonio's first poster had various religious drawings with a message at the top which stated, "The only way to save the world." The obvious implication from Antonio's viewpoint is that God is the only way to save the environment. The teacher rejected the poster because it was religious. Antonio was confused and hurt. He drew a second poster. This poster contained a crayon drawing of stick people depositing trash in a garbage can, others putting trash in a recycle bin, the world with cutout children holding hands and circling the globe, and a picture on the left side of the poster of a robed man kneeling down on one knee with both hands stretched forth to the sky. Antonio clearly understood this person to be Jesus. When he handed in this poster, it was displayed in the cafeteria with the posters of the other four kindergarten classes of approximately eighty students. However, Antonio's poster, unlike the other students, was folded in half so that the picture of Jesus could not be seen. The school teacher took the position that she could not display the poster because it was religious. The principal and the superintendent refused to budge and Liberty Counsel was forced to file a federal lawsuit.

In Homestead, Florida, Reverend Kenneth Greathouse sought to establish a new church called Apostolic Worship Center. He was temporarily renting space in a storefront business district. He was told he had to leave the facilities or otherwise face fines because the code was being redrafted. The city redrafted its zoning code so that churches coming into the business district can only reside there for a maximum of two years. After that, the churches needed to move and the location could never again be used by any religious institution. When the city refused to repeal this unconstitutional ordinance, Liberty Counsel filed suit — and won, I might add.

College students who attend the Miami-Dade Community College set aside one week toward the end of the summer to pass out a business-sized card containing the following message: "The call you'll never forget." Underneath the message was a local telephone number. This number dialed their local church, where the caller would receive a voice-recorded message of the Gospel. The students wanted to hand out these cards to other students on campus during non-class time. To their surprise, they were confronted by college security officers and were told that they could not hand out the cards on campus. The students could not believe this was happening. The students returned on the following day to pass out the cards and again were confronted by security officers. This time the officers phoned a police officer who threatened arrest if they continued to hand out the cards. Liberty Counsel filed suit on behalf of the students and won this case too.

In Missouri and Louisiana, public school students were told they could not pass out the Truth for Youth Bible to fellow classmates during the annual "See You at the Pole" event. Fortunately, Liberty Counsel was able to intervene in both of these matters to resolve them. One was resolved on the eve of the event short of litigation, but the other required a federal lawsuit.

When Joshua Burton was in the fourth grade, he brought his Bible to school to read on a bench by himself before the beginning of the school day. The teacher told him he could not bring his Bible to school because of the "separation of church and state." When

Joshua told his father, his father thought this must be a misunderstanding and surely Joshua could bring his Bible to school. On another day, Joshua did bring his Bible to school, and even though he had the Bible closed and did not read it, the teacher approached him and, in front of the class, took his Bible and then escorted Joshua to the cafeteria where he had to stay in detention all day, solely for bringing his Bible to school.

I could list hundreds and hundreds of examples of religious discrimination that we have handled at Liberty Counsel. Some of these situations are so bizarre you would think they are a creation of someone's wild imagination. We have been surprised to determine after investigation that rampant discrimination is taking place all across America. Part of the discrimination is based upon an ignorance of the Constitution. The mantra of "separation of church and state" has been repeated so many times that most people understand it to mean that religious faith and practice must be cleansed from the public. Some believe that the only place for religion is within the four walls of the church or possibly in the closet. Fortunately, most of these situations resolve through education. However, the cases that we encounter are simply the tip of the iceberg. Those instances which do not resolve through education oftentimes require litigation. Our liberties hang in a delicate balance and we must be vigilant to protect them at all cost.

As a result of this constitutional schizophrenia sucking religion from our public schools, America has developed quite a track record. This track record is not only graced with a dumbing down of our students, it is now laced with a trail of blood. The following illustrates a startling trend in our public school system.

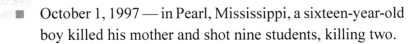

# TAKE BACK AMERICA

- October 1, 1997 — in Pearl, Mississippi, a sixteen-year-old boy killed his mother and shot nine students, killing two.

- December 1, 1997 — in Paducah, Kentucky, while students were leaving a Bible Club prayer meeting on school campus, a fourteen-year-old boy shot and killed three fellow students and wounded five others.

- March 24, 1998 — in Jonesboro, Arkansas, two boys, ages eleven and thirteen, opened fire killing four girls and a teacher, wounding ten others.

- April 24, 1998 — in Edinboro, Pennsylvania, a fourteen-year-old student shot to death a science teacher in front of other students at an eighth grade dance.

- May 19, 1998 — in Fayetteville, Tennessee, an eighteen-year-old honor student opened fire in a high school parking lot, killing a classmate who was dating his ex-girlfriend.

- April 16, 1999 — in Notus, Idaho, a tenth grade student opened fire in a school hallway. Fortunately, no one was injured.

- April 20, 1999 — in Littleton, Colorado, two boys, ages seventeen and eighteen, shot and killed twelve classmates and one teacher, wounding twenty-three others before killing themselves. Many of these shootings were religiously motivated. The gunmen asked some of the students whether they believed in Jesus. When the students said yes, the gunmen murdered them.

- April 22, 1999 — in Scotlandville, Louisiana, a fourteen-year-old fired a weapon from a parking lot aiming for a student he had previously argued with, but instead he injured a fourteen-year-old girl standing nearby.

- April 29, 1999 — in Brooklyn, New York, five middle school students were taken into custody on charges of conspiracy to commit murder, arson, and manufacturing explosives. They intended to blow up their school.

- May 20, 1999 — in Conyers, Georgia, a fifteen-year-old student upset over a broken romance opened fire injuring six classmates.

- February 29, 2000 — in Mount Morris Township, Michigan, a first-grade boy shot and killed his six-year-old classmate after the two had an argument.

- May 15, 2001 — in Ennis, Texas, a sophomore, upset over his relationship with a female student, took seventeen hostages in class and ultimately shot and killed the female student and himself.

- January 15, 2002 — in Manhattan, New York, a high school teenager opened fire, seriously wounding two students.

- April 14, 2003 — in New Orleans, Louisiana, four teenagers killed one student and wounded three others by gunfire at their high school.

- November 24, 2004 — in Valparaiso, Indiana, a fifteen-year-old high school student pulled two large knives out of his pants and stabbed seven classmates.

- March 21, 2005 — on the Red Lake Indian reservation in Minnesota, a high school student killed five students, a teacher, and an unarmed security guard before killing himself.

- August 30, 2006 — in Hillsborough, North Carolina, a student opened fire at his high school injuring two students, after shooting his father to death.

- October 10, 2007 — in Cleveland, Ohio, a fourteen-year-old student, who had previously made threats against his peers and the school, shot two teachers and two students before killing himself.

- December 4, 2008 — in Montco, Pennsylvania, a fifteen-year-old boy was institutionalized after stealing three guns and hundreds of rounds of ammunition from his father and plotting to shoot other students and himself.

- May 18, 2009 — in Larose, Louisiana, after an eighth-grade student fired at his teacher for refusing to praise Marilyn Manson and missed, the student went to the bathroom and turned the gun on himself.

- March 12, 2010 — in Brooklyn, Manhattan, and Queens, New York, three different students, in separate events, were stabbed by their peers.

- January 5, 2011 — in Omaha, Nebraska, a student shot the principal and assistant principal of his high school before turning the gun on himself. Both the student and the assistant principal died.

The bloody list could go on ad infinitum. It doesn't take a rocket scientist to figure out what is happening in America. Noah

Webster clearly understood what would happen when we remove God from the basis of our government. He penned the following words in 1836:

> The moral principles and concepts contained in the Scriptures ought to form the basis of all our civil constitutions and laws…All the miseries and evils which man may suffer from vice, crime, ambition, injustice, oppression, slavery and war, perceived from their disguising or neglecting the precepts contained in the Bible.[29]

Addressing public school teachers in 1995, Harvard professor Chester M. Pierce told the teachers:

> Every child in America entering school at the age of five is insane because he comes to school with certain allegiances towards our founding fathers, toward his parents, toward a belief in a supernatural being…. It is up to you teachers to make all of these sick children well by creating the International Children of the Future.[30]

We have reaped what we have sown. God has given us a choice. We can choose His blessings or we can reap the curses. It appears that we are reaping the inevitable results of our rejection of God. It's time to take back America.

# CHAPTER 4
## It's Time to Take Back America

We are too late in America's history to remain apathetic or unconcerned. Whether you're a Christian or not, you must admit that America is broken. Something is wrong. The question is how can we fix America? The founders agreed that morality and virtue were necessary to good government. Some religion was better than no religion. The founders chose Judeo-Christian religious principles. Although all of the founders were not orthodox Christians, they nevertheless operated from a Judeo-Christian worldview. Our public schools inculcated morality and virtue. The governed were self-restrained and therefore needed very little external governmental restraint.

History is a good teacher. If we understand the lessons of our history, we don't have to repeat the mistakes of the past. Comparing the American Revolution to the French Revolution should teach us something. Both Revolutions occurred during the same general historical era. Both were concerned with personal liberty. However, the philosophical basis of the two Revolutions was fundamentally different. The American Revolution was based upon Judeo-Christian religion, morality, and virtue. Spiritual liberty was seen as a prerequisite to physical liberty. The founding fathers believed that external liberty was not possible without a precedent of spiritual liberty.

Alexis deTocqueville was the famous French statesman, historian, and social philosopher who toured the United States in 1831. Documenting his observations of America, deTocqueville stated:

> Upon my arrival in the United States the religious aspect of the country was the first thing that struck my attention; and the longer I stayed there, the more I perceived the great political consequences resulting from this new state of things.
>
> In France I had almost always seen the spirit of religion and the spirit of freedom marching in opposite directions. But in America I found they were intimately united and that they reigned in common over the same country.[1]

Unlike the American Revolution, the foundation of the French Revolution was based upon human reason. In contrast to the religious liberty enjoyed in America, the French Revolution suppressed churches and attempted to close them. The churches were used as a means to inculcate human reasoning. In fact, in most dictatorships or communist regimes, churches are the first target. Despotic governments know that in order to lead people like robots, you must kill their spiritual freedom. That's why the former Soviet Union turned traditional churches into museums. This is precisely what occurred during the French Revolution.

The result was not liberty but bloodshed and chaos. Since the American Revolution, America has enjoyed only one government, but since the French Revolution, the French have encountered scores of governmental systems.

The lesson learned from the French and the American Revolutions is that true liberty can only be established if we base our foundation on God and spiritual freedom. When we suppress spiritual freedom and displace God with human reason, the government structure we create will eventually self-destruct. We can have no personal freedom in the absence of spiritual freedom.

During the early birth of this country, there was a critical time where our founders were at a crossroads. If they chose one way, our country would never have been birthed, and if they chose another, it would birth the freest nation on earth. During the early deliberations when the founders gathered to debate what kind of constitution would govern our new society, there were bitter divisions and bickering. The assembly almost deteriorated and broke up, but at that critical moment, Benjamin Franklin stood up in their midst and spoke these now famous words:

The small progress we have made after four or five weeks close attendance and continual reasonings with each other — our different sentiments on almost every question, several of the last producing as many nays as ayes, is methinks a melancholy proof of the imperfection of the Human Understanding. We, indeed, seem to feel our own want of political wisdom, since we have been running about in search of it. We have gone back to ancient history for models of Government, and examined the different forms of those Republics which having been formed with the seeds of their own dissolution now no longer exist. And we have viewed Modern States all around Europe, but find none in their Constitutions suitable to our circumstances.

In this situation of this Assembly, groping as it were in the dark to find political truth, and scarce able to distinguish it when presented to us, how has it happened, Sir, that we have not hitherto once thought of humbly applying to the Father of lights to illuminate our understandings? In the beginning of the Contest with Great Britain, when we were sensible of danger we had daily prayer in this room for the divine protection. Our prayers, Sir, were heard, and they were graciously answered. All of us who were engaged in the struggle must have observed frequent instances of a Superintending providence in our favor. To that kind providence we owe this happy opportunity of consulting in peace on the means of establishing our future national felicity. And have we now forgotten that powerful friend? Or do we imagine that we no longer need his assistance? I have lived, Sir, a long time, and the longer I live, the more convincing proofs I see of this truth — that God governs in the affairs of men. And if a sparrow cannot fall to the ground without his notice, is it probable that an empire can rise without his aid? We have been assured, Sir, in the sacred writings, that "except the Lord build the House they labour in vain that build it."

I firmly believe this; and I also believe that without his concurring aid we shall succeed in this political building no better than the Builders of Babel: We shall be divided by our little partial local interests; our projects will be confounded, and we ourselves shall become a reproach and bye word down to future ages.[2]

Now that our country has been established and we have come through the early period of bloodshed, have we forgotten our most powerful friend, or do we suppose we no longer need Him? "Except the Lord build the house they labor in vain that build it."[3] As Benjamin Franklin noted, if we do not invoke God in our daily lives and make him the foundation of government, we shall succeed in this political building no better than the builders of Babel. We will be divided by our local partial interests. Our projects will be confounded and we will become a reproach to future generations.

In order to take back America, we must have a spiritual revival and we must become involved in our society. Oftentimes when talking about this subject, people take an either/or approach to the matter. Some people tend toward the pietistic side of things and say that the only thing we can do is pray. Others tend to the political power side of the coin and say that we must enact new laws to reflect our values. The truth of the matter is that we must do both. We must pray and we must become active.

Obviously, we are involved in a spiritual battle. The battles and the struggles that we see in the physical realm are simply an outgrowth of the broader spiritual battle going on in the cosmos between Christ and Satan. In the book of Daniel, the prophet had a dream. He was disturbed by the dream and asked God to give him the interpretation. In Chapter 10, verse 4, the angel Gabriel came to Daniel three weeks after he began his prayer for the interpretation of the dream. Gabriel stated to Daniel that God heard his prayer on the very day he prayed and dispensed Gabriel to Daniel to interpret the dream. However, the angel stated that he was delayed for three weeks because he was engaged in a battle against the prince of Persia. In the context of the chapter, the prince of Persia is a spiritual angel over the nation of Persia. Historically, Daniel was a Jewish captive in the nation of Medo-Persia and that country was under siege by the rival nation of Greece. On earth there was a physical battle going on between the nations of Medo-Persia and Greece. The reason the angel Gabriel was delayed is because when he was sent to Daniel, who resided in the nation of Greece, the prince of the opposing nation battled Gabriel. Gabriel had to do battle in the spiritual realm so that he could come to Daniel in the physical realm to interpret the dream.

The point of the chapter is that what we see in the physical realm has a counterpart in the spiritual. Obviously we need to be engaged in prayer on behalf of our country. Prayer is a powerful weapon. The Apostle Paul tells us in the book of Ephesians about spiritual warfare:

> For our struggle is not against flesh and blood, but against the rulers, against the authorities, against the powers in this dark world and against the spiritual forces of evil in the heavenly realms. Therefore put on the full

armor of God, so that when the day of evil comes, you may be able to stand your ground, and after you have done everything, to stand. Stand firm then, with the belt of truth buckled around your waist, with the breastplate of righteousness in place, with your feet fitted with the readiness that comes from the gospel of peace. In addition to all this, take up the shield of faith, with which you can extinguish all the flaming arrows of the evil one. Take the helmet of salvation and the sword of the Spirit, which is the word of God. And pray in the Spirit on all occasions with all kinds of prayers and requests. With this in mind, be alert and always keep on praying for all the saints.[4]

There is no question that we must have spiritual revival in America. We can have every just and perfect law, but if our people don't have a life-changing experience, all of the laws will mean nothing. As John Adams once stated, "Our Constitution was made only for a moral and religious people. It is wholly inadequate to the government of any other."[5]

In addition to prayer and a changed life, we must also have a renewed mind. Our laws must reflect our spiritual renewal. The spiritual liberty must produce physical liberty. As the Declaration of Independence states, governments are instituted primarily for the purpose of protecting our God-given, pre-existing, unalienable rights. If government must protect these God-given liberties, then government must reflect these liberties in its laws and policies. We, therefore, must enact laws that reflect our values. This does not mean that we pass legislation requiring everyone to

believe in a certain way or attend a certain church. However, all of our laws contain some kind of moral judgment. A law against protecting private property is a moral judgment that people have the right to own private property. Our laws against murder contain a moral judgment that life is sacred and murder is wrong. Every law reflects some kind of moral judgment. Simply because the moral judgment happens to be supported by or is coincident with our religious belief is no reason not to have the law. Christians have been intimidated into silence by antireligious organizations stating that Christians are imposing their morality when they enter into the political realm. Certainly Christians are imposing their morality, but someone who is not a Christian is also imposing their morality. All laws contain a moral or an amoral basis. All laws are value judgments. Clearly your Christian faith is not a disability. Obviously, the founders of this country believed that our Christian liberty was essential to good government. In the absence of our spiritual liberty, our physical liberty will obviously fail.

The history of Christianity in this country is like a pendulum. Christian influences have had their ebb and flow. Our public schools originally taught people how to read solely for the purpose of being able to read the Bible. Our public schools inculcated religious instruction for over two hundred years. It was not until the early 1960's that religious morality and teaching in the public schools was ever questioned or challenged by our judicial system. Booting religion out of our public schools is, in fact, a recent phenomenon. Why is it that public schools are such a target of religious controversy? The obvious answer is that in order to change the future of America, the easiest and quickest way is to change the minds of our young people. It only takes two generations of school students (just twenty-four years) to have a profound impact on America.

One recent public school history book contains several pages on Marilyn Monroe and a small short paragraph on George Washington. When our school textbooks rewrite American history and erase from that history our Judeo-Christian heritage, the students learn of a different America than our founding fathers knew. When our students are taught moral relativism, it is no wonder why they pick up a gun and shoot someone for no explainable reason. Most of us have been funneled through the public education system. Certainly there are good Christian teachers and students in the public schools. I am not criticizing them, but we must admit that the system is broken.

The public school system in general is a change agent and it teaches certain values. If the values are not religiously based, then the "values" will be wholly secular. Here again, we get back to the difference between the American and French Revolutions. In a religious-based system, there are absolute values. We are taught that we are made in the image of God and have value. We are also taught that others have value and we must respect them. There are transcendent rights and wrongs. A human-based system really doesn't place much value on humanity since humanity is no different than the animal kingdom. There are no transcendent values in a human-based system since these values change over time and vary from one person to the next. Therefore, there is no absolute right and wrong in the human-based system. A human-based system is a recipe for chaos.

# TAKE BACK AMERICA

To take back America, we must not only be involved in the political system, but we must also be involved in the educational system. We must run for office. We must vote. We must challenge the idea of the public school monopoly.

We must also become educated about our Judeo-Christian beliefs, values, and our history. If we don't know the basis of our government and the reasons for its creation, then every wind of doctrine or new idea articulated by some eloquent speaker will captivate our mind and change our values. Every time we drive on the road we must know the rules of the road. If you don't know the rules of the road, you won't know how to navigate or how fast to drive.

When the fundamental issue at stake is the ability to share the Gospel of Jesus Christ and to change another person's life forever, we must know the rules of our society that either help or hinder us in that endeavor. We must be able to recognize whether these rules or whether the pontifications of those in authority are right or wrong. We must not take legislation at face value, but we must challenge these enactments to determine whether they are correct. For example, if you go to a public library and ask permission to use the common meeting room for a religious meeting, do you simply turn away when you see a policy that says the common room can be used for secular but not religious purposes? If you don't know your liberties, you will turn away and think it strange but not challenge the system. However, if you know your liberties and understand that this religious discrimination policy is fundamentally wrong, you will challenge the system. You will try first to change it in an amicable fashion, but if government won't listen to your reasonable claims, then you have the alternative to use the judicial system as a check on government to bring the system back into line. Remember, the purpose of government is to protect your God-given, pre-existing, unalienable rights. To become informed of these liberties, you need to read and educate yourself. Liberty Counsel has a list of resources to equip you.

We must also stand behind those organizations that are making a difference in America. It is amusing that when we take $100.00 to the mall it seems pretty small, but when we think about giving $100.00 to our church or to a nonprofit organization, it seems like a large contribution. The founding fathers were willing to sacrifice their lives and their fortunes to preserve our liberty. We must be vigilant to preserve our liberty. You may not be able to enter into a courtroom and may not want to, but there are organizations that battle for your freedom every day. Liberty Counsel is one of those organizations. Litigation is oftentimes a necessary activity to protect our freedoms. It is also an expensive endeavor. On one case that we took to the United States Supreme Court, we had to print a two-volume appendix for the Supreme Court. Special printers have to be used for Supreme Court documents. The printing cost alone that we paid to the printer was almost $20,000.00. While the cost of litigation may be high, the cost of surrender is too great to bear.

It is time to take back America. We not only owe it to our founding fathers and ourselves, but we also are obligated to preserve a free America for our children. The task may seem insurmountable. If you are overwhelmed by the prospect, let me remind you of one scene in the Wizard of Oz. You remember when Dorothy and her entourage were nervously walking down the long hallway to see the Wizard. They were intimidated by their surroundings. The booming voice of the Wizard that was accompanied by puffs of smoke was frightening. Some in the group were tempted to turn back and run. When they were nervously huddled together in fear of their lives, little Toto calmly walked up to the curtain behind which the Wizard sat. He gently tugged on the bottom of the curtain and pulled it back. There sat a spindly old man on a chair speaking into a microphone and pushing buttons to magnify his voice and manipulate the smoke. All of a sudden, the fear that once gripped them vanished. The Wizard was not so big after all.

The ACLU and all other antireligious groups are like the Wizard. These groups may huff and puff and intimidate the weak at heart, but we must ask God to pull back the curtain so we can see Him standing by our side. We must boldly move forward in confidence. We must take back America!

## We Have a Choice to "Turn Back" or "Take Back"!

The courage and resolve shown by a young woman from rural Kentucky remains an enduring inspiration to every Christian facing pressure from forces trying to silence their testimony for Christ. Although I touched on her story in this book's Introduction, Megan Chapman's story is worthy of further examination.

Megan had a choice. It's the same choice you and I have. Will we stand for Christ at the moment of testing? Faced with the choice of standing up for Christ or being silenced by the ACLU, Megan chose to stand for Christ!

On the morning of her high school graduation, a federal judge issued an order barring Russell County High School and Megan (she was cited in the order by name!) from conducting prayer during commencement.

Can you imagine the overpowering intimidation a high school senior must feel when reading her name in a federal lawsuit filed by the ACLU? Thankfully, we were able to speak to Megan personally around 4:00 pm, only three hours before her graduation ceremony.

I counseled her that God can turn apparent adversity into great opportunity when you trust and obey Him. Just hours later, more that 3,000 people packed the high school gymnasium to watch 196 seniors graduate. Before the principal finished his opening remarks, the senior class stood as one body to recite The Lord's Prayer!

The result? Thunderous applause erupted and drowned out the end of the prayer! Some students were so overcome with emotion they could not even finish the prayer.

Then, Megan Chapman came to the podium prepared only to deliver a secular poem, *The Road Less Traveled*. But when Megan looked out at the large audience, she asked God to give her a message. She realized that she was not put in this position to bow down to the ACLU and merely recite a secular poem!

She put away the poem and spoke from her heart. Megan began by sharing how God had led her since she was a child. She spoke of the peace she has encountered since giving her life to Jesus.

And she wished her classmates the same peace that can only come from a personal relationship with Jesus Christ.

Megan's speech was repeatedly interrupted with applause and punctuated by several standing ovations. The Louisville *Courier-Journal* journalist covering the event described the evening as having a "revival-like atmosphere," to the complete dismay of the ACLU!

The following morning, we received a call from Fox News, and on Saturday night Megan shared her story about her personal salvation through Jesus Christ — with millions of viewers!

That same afternoon, I spoke with Dr. Jerry Falwell, Founder of Liberty University, and he authorized me to offer Megan a full scholarship to join the 2006 freshman class at Liberty University! When I shared the good news with Megan, she was overcome by tearful amazement.

"Are you kidding?" she said. "I've been praying for several years to be able to attend Liberty University, but I simply could not afford it." But to my bewilderment, she did not immediately accept the offer. I was puzzled.

I called her on Monday and a voice that sounded just like Megan answered the phone. "Megan?" I asked. "No, this is Mandy, her twin sister," the voice replied. Mandy, it turned out, was the one who gave her classmates a bookmark with the Lord's Prayer just in case some forgot the words.

I called Dr. Falwell. "Guess what," I said, "Megan has a twin sister!" Dr. Falwell briefly paused to reflect on this new development, and then offered Mandy a full scholarship! Mandy couldn't believe it! They both enrolled at Liberty University.

But there's even more to the story. When CNN Headline News called wanting to feature Liberty Counsel in their series "God's Warriors," we introduced CNN correspondent Christiane Amenpour to the twins. The story of Megan and Mandy and their faith has now been shown several times around the world in the two hour documentary called "God's Christian Warriors." Megan and Mandy have received emails and notes of appreciation from all over the world!

The last TV appearance for Dr. Falwell before he went to be with the Lord on May 15, 2007, was "God's Christian Warriors." Megan and Mandy also have the unique distinction of being featured on the front page of the last *National Liberty Journal* newspaper published by Dr. Falwell while he was alive. And the last *Falwell Confidential* email Jerry Falwell sent out featured the story of Megan and Mandy Chapman.

God loves irony. Megan had a choice — buckle to the pressure of the ACLU or stand up for Christ. Had she buckled, her graduation would have been silent and her life would have taken a different direction. But, she stood for Christ, and her witness was heard around the country.

The first twenty minutes of the two-hour CNN documentary is devoted to Liberty Counsel and Liberty University School of Law. During this twenty-minute segment, the documentary features Dr. Jerry Falwell and covers the the rise of the Moral Majority and Christian political activism. The documentary then covers the rise of Liberty Counsel and Liberty University School of Law. Chrstiane correctly points out my design of the Supreme Courtroom at the law school, which is intended to be a clone of the United States Supreme Court. It is here we will train future activists, including legal advocates, judges, and political leaders.

Christiane then interviews Megan and Mandy Chapman. As a second semester freshman at that time, Megan tells Christiane that she wants to become a lawyer so she can defend religious liberties and overturn *Roe v. Wade*, the 1973 Supreme Court decision that purported to "legalize" abortion on demand.

Winning the coveted George Foster Peabody Award and the Television Academy Honors, this documentary has been repeatedly aired around the world multiple times. The twins could never have imagined that their Christian testimony would go global.

On the walls at Liberty Counsel and Liberty University School of Law hang four picture frames depicting the last "Falwell Confidential" email sent by Dr. Falwell, the last television interview, the last print media interview and the last edition of the *National Liberty Journal* when Dr. Falwell was alive, of which he was editor and publisher. The Falwell Confidential email is about Megan and Mandy Chapman and Liberty Counsel. The last television media interview is the one mentioned, "God's Christian Warriors," and the last *National Liberty Journal* features on the cover Dr. Falwell, Megan and Mandy Chapman and me, featuring the article I wrote about this case called "Silence is Not an Option."

In May 2010, Megan and Mandy graduated from college at Liberty University. In August 2010, Megan began her legal education at Liberty University School of Law. God willing, in May 2012, I will have the honor of placing the Juris Doctor hood on Megan and commissioning her to go do battle against the ACLU.

Megan had a choice. It is the same choice each of us face. She could have compromised and remained silent in the face of opposition. After all, her peers knew she was a Christian. She had a federal court order naming her specifically. She had never been in trouble and she had no desire to begin now. It was just a short prayer anyway. She was already enrolled in another college. But, when Megan walked to that podium she did not flinch. Compromise was not an option she considered. God did not call her to that moment to be a coward or to read a secular poem. At that moment of decision, she chose to stand for Christ regardless of the consequences.

Megan and Mandy experienced a "Back to the Future" kind of moment where one decision would take them in one direction and another would take them on a completely different tangent. They were faithful, and God has used them in ways that they never could have imagined. This is the same choice we all face. When we remain faithful to Christ, all we need to do is buckle up and enjoy the ride. It's time we all buckle up and take back America.

CITIZEN BALLOT
☐ President
☐ Senate
☐ House

# APPENDIX A
## Deuteronomy 28

1 If you fully obey the LORD your God and carefully follow all his commands I give you today, the LORD your God will set you high above all the nations on earth.

2 All these blessings will come upon you and accompany you if you obey the LORD your God:

3 You will be blessed in the city and blessed in the country.

4 The fruit of your womb will be blessed, and the crops of your land and the young of your livestock  the calves of your herds and the lambs of your flocks.

5 Your basket and your kneading trough will be blessed.

6 You will be blessed when you come in and blessed when you go out.

7 The LORD will grant that the enemies who rise up against you will be defeated before you. They will come at you from one direction but flee from you in seven.

8 The LORD will send a blessing on your barns and on every-

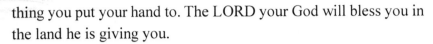

thing you put your hand to. The LORD your God will bless you in the land he is giving you.

9 The LORD will establish you as his holy people, as he promised you on oath, if you keep the commands of the LORD your God and walk in his ways.

10 Then all the peoples on earth will see that you are called by the name of the LORD, and they will fear you.

11 The LORD will grant you abundant prosperity in the fruit of your womb, the young of your livestock and the crops of your ground in the land he swore to your forefathers to give you.

12 The LORD will open the heavens, the storehouse of his bounty, to send rain on your land in season and to bless all the work of your hands. You will lend to many nations but will borrow from none.

13 The LORD will make you the head, not the tail. If you pay attention to the commands of the LORD your God that I give you this day and carefully follow them, you will always be at the top, never at the bottom.

14 Do not turn aside from any of the commands I give you today, to the right or to the left, following other gods and serving them.

15 However, if you do not obey the LORD your God and do not carefully follow all his commands and decrees I am giving you today, all these curses will come upon you and overtake you:

16 You will be cursed in the city and cursed in the country.

17 Your basket and your kneading trough will be cursed.

18  The fruit of your womb will be cursed, and the crops of your land, and the calves of your herds and the lambs of your flocks.

19  You will be cursed when you come in and cursed when you go out.

20  The LORD will send on you curses, confusion and rebuke in everything you put your hand to, until you are destroyed and come to sudden ruin because of the evil you have done in forsaking him.

21  The LORD will plague you with diseases until he has destroyed you from the land you are entering to possess.

22  The LORD will strike you with wasting disease, with fever and inflammation, with scorching heat and drought, with blight and mildew, which will plague you until you perish.

23  The sky over your head will be bronze, the ground beneath you iron.

24  The LORD will turn the rain of your country into dust and powder; it will come down from the skies until you are destroyed.

25  The LORD will cause you to be defeated before your enemies. You will come at them from one direction but flee from them in seven, and you will become a thing of horror to all the kingdoms on earth.

26  Your carcasses will be food for all the birds of the air and the beasts of the earth, and there will be no one to frighten them away.

27  The LORD will afflict you with the boils of Egypt and with tumors, festering sores and the itch, from which you cannot be cured.

28  The LORD will afflict you with madness, blindness and confusion of mind.

29  At midday you will grope about like a blind man in the dark. You will be unsuccessful in everything you do; day after day you will be oppressed and robbed, with no one to rescue you.

30  You will be pledged to be married to a woman, but another will take her and ravish her. You will build a house, but you will not live in it. You will plant a vineyard, but you will not even begin to enjoy its fruit.

31  Your ox will be slaughtered before your eyes, but you will eat none of it. Your donkey will be forcibly taken from you and will not be returned. Your sheep will be given to your enemies, and no one will rescue them.

32  Your sons and daughters will be given to another nation, and you will wear out your eyes watching for them day after day, powerless to lift a hand.

33  A people that you do not know will eat what your land and labor produce, and you will have nothing but cruel oppression all your days.

34  The sights you see will drive you mad.

35  The LORD will afflict your knees and legs with painful boils that cannot be cured, spreading from the soles of your feet to the top of your head.

36 The LORD will drive you and the king you set over you to a nation unknown to you or your fathers. There you will worship other gods, gods of wood and stone.

37 You will become a thing of horror and an object of scorn and ridicule to all the nations where the LORD will drive you.

38 You will sow much seed in the field but you will harvest little, because locusts will devour it.

39 You will plant vineyards and cultivate them but you will not drink the wine or gather the grapes, because worms will eat them.

40 You will have olive trees throughout your country but you will not use the oil, because the olives will drop off.

41 You will have sons and daughters but you will not keep them, because they will go into captivity.

42 Swarms of locusts will take over all your trees and the crops of your land.

43 The alien who lives among you will rise above you higher and higher, but you will sink lower and lower.

44 He will lend to you, but you will not lend to him. He will be the head, but you will be the tail.

45 All these curses will come upon you. They will pursue you and overtake you until you are destroyed, because you did not obey the LORD your God and observe the commands and decrees he gave you.

46 They will be a sign and a wonder to you and your descendants forever.

47  Because you did not serve the LORD your God joyfully and gladly in the time of prosperity,

48  therefore in hunger and thirst, in nakedness and dire poverty, you will serve the enemies the LORD sends against you. He will put an iron yoke on your neck until he has destroyed you.

49  The LORD will bring a nation against you from far away, from the ends of the earth, like an eagle swooping down, a nation whose language you will not understand,

50  a fierce looking nation without respect for the old or pity for the young.

51  They will devour the young of your livestock and the crops of your land until you are destroyed. They will leave you no grain, new wine or oil, nor any calves of your herds or lambs of your flocks until you are ruined.

52  They will lay siege to all the cities throughout your land until the high fortified walls in which you trust fall down. They will besiege all the cities throughout the land the LORD your God is giving you.

53  Because of the suffering that your enemy will inflict on you during the siege, you will eat the fruit of the womb, the flesh of the sons and daughters the LORD your God has given you.

54  Even the most gentle and sensitive man among you will have no compassion on his own brother or the wife he loves or his surviving children,

55  and he will not give to one of them any of the flesh of his children that he is eating. It will be all he has left because of the

suffering your enemy will inflict on you during the siege of all your cities.

56 The most gentle and sensitive woman among you  so sensitive and gentle that she would not venture to touch the ground with the sole of her foot will begrudge the husband she loves and her own son or daughter

57 the afterbirth from her womb and the children she bears. For she intends to eat them secretly during the siege and in the distress that your enemy will inflict on you in your cities.

58 If you do not carefully follow all the words of this law, which are written in this book, and do not revere this glorious and awesome name the LORD your God,

59 the LORD will send fearful plagues on you and your descendants, harsh and prolonged disasters, and severe and lingering illnesses.

60 He will bring upon you all the diseases of Egypt that you dreaded, and they will cling to you.

61 The LORD will also bring on you every kind of sickness and disaster not recorded in this Book of the Law, until you are destroyed.

62 You who were as numerous as the stars in the sky will be left but few in number, because you did not obey the LORD your God.

63 Just as it pleased the LORD to make you prosper and increase in number, so it will please him to ruin and destroy you. You will be uprooted from the land you are entering to possess.

64 Then the LORD will scatter you among all nations, from one end of the earth to the other. There you will worship other gods—gods of wood and stone, which neither you nor your fathers have known.

65 Among those nations you will find no repose, no resting place for the sole of your foot. There the LORD will give you an anxious mind, eyes weary with longing, and a despairing heart.

66 You will live in constant suspense, filled with dread both night and day, never sure of your life.

67 In the morning you will say, "If only it were evening!" and in the evening, "If only it were morning!" because of the terror that will fill your hearts and the sights that your eyes will see.

68 The LORD will send you back in ships to Egypt on a journey I said you should never make again. There you will offer yourselves for sale to your enemies as male and female slaves, but no one will buy you.[1]

# APPENDIX B
## Declaration of Independence

In Congress, July 4, 1776

The Unanimous Declaration of the Thirteen United States of America

When in the Course of human events it becomes necessary for one people to dissolve the political bands which have connected them with another, and to assume among the Powers of the earth, the separate and equal station to which the Laws of Nature and of Nature's God entitle them, a decent respect to the opinions of mankind requires that they should declare the causes which impel them to the separation.

We hold these truths to be self-evident, that all men are created equal, that they are endowed by their Creator with certain unalienable Rights, that among these are Life, Liberty and the pursuit of Happiness. That to secure these rights, Governments are instituted among Men, deriving their just powers from the consent of the governed, That whenever any Form of Government becomes destructive of these ends, it is the Right of the

People to alter or to abolish it, and to institute new Government, laying its foundation on such principles and organizing its powers in such form, as to them shall seem most likely to affect their Safety and Happiness. Prudence, indeed, will dictate that Governments long established should not be changed for light and transient causes; and accordingly all experience hath shown, that mankind are more disposed to suffer, while evils are sufferable, than to right themselves by abolishing the forms to which they are accustomed. But when a long train of abuses and usurpations, pursuing invariably the same Object evinces a design to reduce them under absolute Despotism, it is their right, it is their duty, to throw off such Government, and to provide new Guards for their future security. Such has been the patient sufferance of these Colonies; and such is now the necessity which constrains them to alter their former Systems of Government. The history of the present King of Great Britain is a history of repeated injuries and usurpations, all having in direct object the establishment of an absolute Tyranny over these States. To prove this, let Facts be submitted to a candid world.

He has refused his Assent to Laws, the most wholesome and necessary for the public good.

He has forbidden his Governors to pass Laws of immediate and pressing importance, unless suspended in their operation till his Assent should be obtained; and when so suspended, he has utterly neglected to attend to them.

He has refused to pass other Laws for the accommodation of large districts of people, unless those people would relinquish the right of Representation in the Legislature, a right inestimable to them and formidable to tyrants only.

He has called together legislative bodies at places unusual, uncomfortable, and distant from the depository of their Public Records, for the sole purpose of fatiguing them into compliance with his measures.

He has dissolved Representative Houses repeatedly, for opposing with manly firmness his invasions on the rights of the people.

He has refused for a long time, after such dissolutions, to cause others to be elected; whereby the Legislative Powers, incapable of Annihilation, have returned to the People at large for their exercise; the State remaining in the mean time exposed to all the dangers of invasion from without, and convulsions within.

He has endeavored to prevent the population of these States; for that purpose obstructing the Laws for Naturalization of Foreigners; refusing to pass others to encourage their migration hither, and raising the conditions of new Appropriations of Lands.

He has obstructed the Administration of Justice, by refusing his Assent to Laws for establishing Judiciary Powers.

He has made Judges dependent on his Will alone, for the tenure of their offices, and the amount and payment of their salaries.

He has erected a multitude of New Offices, and sent hither swarms of Officers to harass our People, and eat out their substance.

He has kept among us, in times of peace, Standing Armies without the Consent of our Legislature.

He has affected to render the Military independent of and superior to the Civil Power.

He has combined with others to subject us to a jurisdiction foreign to our constitution, and unacknowledged by our laws; giving his Assent to their acts of pretended Legislation:

For quartering large bodies of armed troops among us:

For protecting them, by a mock Trial, from Punishment for any Murders which they should commit on the Inhabitants of these States:

For cutting off our Trade with all parts of the world:

For imposing taxes on us without our Consent:

For depriving us in many cases, of the benefits of Trial by Jury:

For transporting us beyond Seas to be tried for pretended offenses:

For abolishing the free System of English Laws in a neighboring Province, establishing therein an Arbitrary government, and enlarging its Boundaries so as to render it at once an example and fit instrument for introducing the same absolute rule into these Colonies:

For taking away our Charters, abolishing our most valuable Laws, and altering fundamentally the Forms of our Government:

For suspending our own Legislature, and declaring themselves invested with Power to legislate for us in all cases whatsoever.

He has abdicated Government here, by declaring us out of his Protection and waging War against us.

He has plundered our seas, ravaged our Coasts, burnt our towns, and destroyed the lives of our people.

He is at this time transporting large armies of foreign mercenaries to compleat the works of death, desolation and tyranny, already begun with circumstances of Cruelty & perfidy scarcely paralleled in the most barbarous ages, and totally unworthy the Head of a civilized nation.

He has constrained our fellow Citizens taken Captive on the high Seas to bear Arms against their Country, to become the executioners of their friends and Brethren, or to fall themselves by their Hands.

He has excited domestic insurrections amongst us, and has endeavored to bring on the inhabitants of our frontiers, the merciless Indian Savages, whose known rule of warfare, is an undistinguished destruction of all ages, sexes and conditions.

In every stage of these Oppressions We have Petitioned for Redress in the most humble terms: Our repeated Petitions have been answered only by repeated injury. A Prince, whose character is thus marked by every act which may define a Tyrant, is unfit to be the ruler of a free People.

Nor have We been wanting in attention to our British brethren. We have warned them from time to time of attempts by their legislature to extend an unwarrantable jurisdiction over us. We have reminded them of the circumstances of our emigration and settlement here. We have appealed to their native justice and magnanimity, and we have conjured them by the ties of our common kindred to disavow these usurpations, which would inevitably interrupt our connections and correspondence. They too have been deaf to the voice of justice and consanguinity. We must, therefore, acquiesce in the necessity, which denounces our Separation, and hold them, as we hold the rest of mankind, Enemies in War, in Peace Friends.

We, therefore, the Representatives of the United States of America, in General Congress, Assembled, appealing to the Supreme Judge of the world for the rectitude of our intentions, do, in the Name, and by Authority of the good People of these Colonies, solemnly publish and declare, That these United Colonies are, and of Right ought to be Free and Independent States; that they are Absolved from all Allegiance to the British Crown, and that all political connection between them and the State of Great Britain, is and ought to be totally dissolved; and that as Free and Independent States, they have full Power to levy War, conclude Peace, contract Alliances, establish Commerce, and to do all other Acts and Things which Independent States may of right do. And for the support of this Declaration, with a firm reliance on the Protection of Divine Providence, we mutually pledge to each other our Lives, our Fortunes and our sacred Honor.

**Connecticut:**

Roger Sherman

William Williams

Samuel Huntington

Oliver Wolcott

**Delaware:**

Caesar Rodney

Thomas McKean

George Read

**Georgia:**

Button Gwinnett

George Walton

Lyman Hall

**Maryland:**

Samuel Chase

Thomas Stone

William Paca

Charles Carroll of Carrollton

**Massachusetts:**

John Hancock

Samuel Adams

Robert Treat Paine

John Adams

Elbridge Gerry

**New Hampshire:**

Josiah Bartlett

Matthew Thornton

William Whipple

**New Jersey:**

Richard Stockton

John Hart

John Witherspoon

Abraham Clark

Francis Hopkinson

**New York:**

William Floyd

Francis Lewis

Philip Livingston

Lewis Morris

**North Carolina:**

William Hooper

John Penn

Joseph Hewes

**Pennsylvania:**

Robert Morris

James Smith

Benjamin Rush

George Taylor

Benjamin Franklin

James Wilson

John Morton

George Ross

George Clymer

**Rhode Island:**

Stephen Hopkins

William Ellery

**South Carolina:**

Edward Rutledge

Thomas Lynch, Jr.

Thomas Heyward, Jr.

Arthur Middleton

**Virginia:**

George Wythe

Thomas Nelson, Jr.

Richard Henry Lee

Francis Lightfoot Lee

Thomas Jefferson

Benjamin Harrison

Carter Braxton

# APPENDIX C
## Eighth Grade Final Exam

C ontained below is a final exam given to eighth grade students in Salina, Kansas, in 1895. The exam is taken from the original document on file at the Smoky Valley Genealogical Society and Library in Salina, Kansas, and reprinted by the *Salina Journal* on July 7, 2000. See http://www.saljournal.com.

### 8th Grade Final Exam: Salina, Kansas — 1895

*Grammar (Time, 1 hour)*

1. Give nine rules for the use of Capital Letters.

2. Name the Parts of Speech and define those that have no modifications.

3. Define Verse, Stanza and Paragraph.

4. What are the Principal Parts of a verb? Give Principal Parts of do, lie, lay and run.

5. Define Case. Illustrate each Case.

6. What is Punctuation? Give rules for principal marks of Punctuation.

7. Write a composition of about 150 words and show therein that you understand the practical use of the rules of grammar.

## Arithmetic (Time, 1½ hours)

1. Name and define the Fundamental Rules of Arithmetic.
2. A wagon box is 2 feet deep, 10 feet long and 3 feet wide. How many bushels of wheat will it hold?
3. If a load of wheat weighs 3,942 lbs., what is it worth at 50 cts. Per bu., deducting 1,050 lbs. for tare?
4. District No. 33 has a valuation of $35,000. What is the necessary levy to carry on a school seven months at $50 per month, and have $104 for incidentals?
5. Find the cost of 6,720 lbs. coal at $6.00 per ton.
6. Find the interest of $512.60 for 8 months and 18 days at 7 percent.
7. What is the cost of 40 boards 12 inches wide and 16 feet long at $20 per inch?
8. Find the bank discount on $300 for 90 days (no grace) at 10 percent.
9. What is the cost of a square farm at $15 per acre, the distance around which is 640 rods?
10. Write a Bank Check, a Promissory Note, and a Receipt.

## U.S. History (Time, 45 minutes)

1. Give the epochs into which U.S. History is divided.
2. Give an account of the discovery of America by Columbus.
3. Relate the causes and results of the Revolutionary War.

4. Show the territorial growth of the United States.

5. Tell what you can of the history of Kansas.

6. Describe three of the most prominent battles of the Rebellion.

7. Who were the following: Morse, Whitney, Fulton, Bell, Lincoln, Penn, and Howe?

8. Name events connected with the following dates: 1607, 1620, 1800, 1849, and 1865.

## Orthography (Time, 1 hour)

1. What is meant by the following: Alphabet, phonetic, orthography, etymology, and syllabication?

2. What are elementary sounds? How classified?

3. What are the following, and give examples of each: Trigraph, subvocals, diphthong, cognate letters, linguals?

4. Give four substitutes for caret "u."

5. Give two rules for spelling words with final "e." Name two exceptions under each rule.

6. Give two uses of silent letters in spelling. Illustrate each.

7. Define the following prefixes and use in connection with a word: Bi, dis, mis, pre, semi, post, non, inter, mono, super.

8. Mark diacritically and divide into syllables the following, and name the sign that indicates the sound: Card, ball, mercy, sir, odd, cell, rise, blood, fare, last.

9. Use the following correctly in sentences: cite, site, sight, fane, fain, feign, vane, vain, vein, raze, raise, rays.

10. Write 10 words frequently mispronounced and indicate pronunciation by use of diacritical marks and by syllabication.

# TAKE BACK AMERICA

*Geography (Time, 1 hour)*

1. What is climate? Upon what does climate depend?
2. How do you account for the extremes of climate in Kansas?
3. Of what use are rivers? Of what use is the ocean?
4. Describe the mountains of North America.
5. Name and describe the following: Monrovia, Odessa, Denver, Manitoba, Hecla, Yukon, St. Helena, Juan Fermandez, Aspinwall and Orinoco.
6. Name and locate the principal trade centers of the U.S.
7. Name all the republics of Europe and give capital of each.
8. Why is the Atlantic Coast colder than the Pacific in the same latitude?
9. Describe the process by which the water of the ocean returns to the sources of rivers.
10. Describe the movements of the earth. Give inclination of the earth.

# ENDNOTES

## Chapter 2

[1] Letter from Thomas Jefferson to Henry Lee, May 8, 1825, *reprinted in William J. Bennett*, ed., OUR SACRED HONOR 318.

[2] *The Church of the Holy Trinity v. United States*, 143 U.S. 457, 466 (1892).

[3] *Ibid.* at 471.

[4] Washington, Farewell Address, September 17, 1796, *reprinted in* Johnson, GEORGE WASHINGTON THE CHRISTIAN 217-18.

[5] J. Wingate Thornton, THE PULPIT OF THE AMERICAN REVOLUTION (1860) (*reprinted by* Burt Franklin, NY 1970) XXIX.

[6] John Adams, Letter "To the Officers of the First Brigade of the Third Division of the Militia of Massachusetts," October 11, 1798, *reprinted in* Bennett, OUR SACRED HONOR 370 (emphasis added).

[7] Ord. of 1789, July 13, 1789, Art. A III, *reprinted in* DOCUMENTS ILLUS- TRATIVE OF THE FORMATION OF THE UNION OF AMERICAN STATES 52 (1927).

[8] Benjamin Rush, ESSAYS, LITERARY, MORAL, AND PHILOSOPHICAL 93-94 (1806).

[9] David Barton, EDUCATION AND THE FOUNDING FATHERS 4.

[10] William J. Federer, AMERICA'S GOD AND COUNTRY ENCYCLOPEDIA OF QUOTATIONS 282.

[11] Barton, EDUCATION AND THE FOUNDING FATHERS 7.

¹² In order to underscore the dumbing down of America, see Appendix C. Contained therein is a final exam from 1895 given to eighth grade students in Salina, Kansas.

¹³ Barton, EDUCATION AND THE FOUNDING FATHERS 14-15.

## Chapter 3

¹ Ord. of 1789, July 13, 1789, Art. A III, *reprinted in* DOCUMENTS ILLUSTRATIVE OF THE FORMATION OF THE UNION OF AMERICAN STATES 52 (1927).

² *Hyde v. United States*, 225 U.S. 347, 384 (1912) (Holmes, J., dissenting).

³ *See Everson v. Bd. of Educ.*, 330 U.S. 1 (1947). *See also McCollum v. Bd. of Educ.*, 333 U.S. 203, 211 (1948).

⁴ Thomas Jefferson to Messrs. Nehemiah Dodge, Ephraim Robbins and Stephen S. Nelson, a Committee of the Danbury Baptist Association in the State of Connecticut, January 1, 1802, Presidential Papers Microfilm, THOMAS JEFFERSON PAPERS, Manuscript Division, Library of Congress, Ser. I, reel 25, November. 15, 1801 — March 31, 1802; Jefferson to William Johnson, June 12, 1823, Presidential Papers Microfilm, THOMAS JEFFERSON PAPERS, Manuscript Division, Library of Congress, Ser. I, reel 70. The letters referenced herein can be found at the above citation.

⁵ Daniel Dreisbach, *"Sowing Useful Truths and Principles": The Danbury Baptists, Thomas Jefferson, and the "Wall of Separation,"* 39 JOURNAL OF CHURCH AND STATE 455, 459 (1997).

⁶ *Ibid.* at 460.

⁷ *Ibid.*

⁸ *Ibid.* at 462.

⁹ *Ibid.* at 463 n. 16.

¹⁰ *Ibid.* at 465.

¹¹ *Ibid.* at 466.

¹² *Ibid.* at 462 n. 13.

¹³ Thomas Jefferson to the Reverend Samuel Miller, January 23, 1808, in Andrew A. Lipscomb *et al.*, eds., THE WRITINGS OF THOMAS JEFFERSON 11:428;

Jefferson, Second Inaugural Address, March 4, 1805, in Andrew A. Lipscomb *et al.*, eds., THE WRITINGS OF THOMAS JEFFERSON 3:378.

[14] Thomas Jefferson to the Reverend Samuel Miller, January 23, 1808, in THE WRITINGS OF THOMAS JEFFERSON 11:428.

[15] *Ibid.* at 11:430.

[16] J. Body, ed., THE PAPERS OF JEFFERSON 1:105.

[17] *Report of the Committee of Revisors Appointed by the General Assembly of Virginia in MDCCLXXVI* (Richmond, Va., 1984) 59-60; Julian P. Boyd, *et al.*, eds., THE PAPERS OF THOMAS JEFFERSON 2:556.

[18] In the Kentucky-Virginia Resolutions of 1798, Jefferson wrote that the powers not delegated to the United States are reserved to the States and that "no power over the freedom of religion, freedom of speech, or freedom of the press being delegated to the United States by the Constitution, nor prohibited by it to the States, all lawful powers respecting the same did of right remain, and were reserved to the States, or to the people. . . [and are] withheld from the cognizance of federal tribunals." THE KENTUCKY-VIRGINIA RESOLUTIONS AND MR. MADISON'S REPORT OF 1799 2-3.

[19] *See Cantwell v. Connecticut*, 310 U.S. 296 (1940).

[20] *See Everson*, 330 U.S. at 1.

[21] One of the early Supreme Court Justices, Joseph Story, wrote that "the whole power over the subject of religion is left exclusively to the state governments, to be acted upon according to their own sense of justice, and the state constitutions..." J. Story, COMMENTARIES ON THE CONSTITUTION § 1879 (1833).

[22] *Wallace v. Jaffree*, 472 U.S. 38, 106 (Rehnquist, J., dissenting).

[23] Daniel Dreisbach, *Thomas Jefferson and the Danbury Baptists Revisited*, 56:4 WILLIAM AND MARY QUARTERLY 805, 812 (1999).

[24] *School Dist. of Abington Township v. Schempp*, 374 U.S. 203, 209 (1963).

[25] *Stone v. Graham*, 449 U.S. 39 (1980).

[26] *Ibid.* at 42.

[27] *Pfeifer v. City of West Allis*, 91 F. Supp.2d 1253 (E.D. Wis. 2000).

[28] 206 F.3d 1070 (11th Cir. 2000) (en banc).

[29] Noah Webster, HISTORY OF THE UNITED STATES 309-10.

[30] Berit Kjos, BRAVE NEW SCHOOLS 161.

## Chapter 4

[1] Alexis deTocqueville, DEMOCRACY IN AMERICA 1:319.

[2] Benjamin Franklin, Invocation for Prayer at the Constitutional Convention, June 28, 1787, *reprinted in* William Bennett, OUR SACRED HONOR 383-385.

[3] Psalm 127:1.

[4] Ephesians 6:12-18.

[5] John Adams, Letter "To the officers of the First Brigade of the Third Division of the Militia of Massachusetts," October 11, 1798, *reprinted in* Bennett, OUR SACRED HONOR 370.

## Appendix A

[1] Scripture taken from the HOLY BIBLE, NEW INTERNATIONAL VERSION. Copyright © 1973, 1978, 1984 by International Bible Society. Used by permission.

# ABOUT THE AUTHOR

M athew D. Staver, Founder and Chairman of Liberty Counsel, has argued in numerous state and federal courts across the country, including the United States Supreme Court. He has testified before Congressional committees regarding public policy issues of national significance.

Mat serves as Dean of Liberty University School of Law and Chairman of Liberty Counsel Action. He is a trustee for the Supreme Court Historical Society. Mat is considered one of the premier constitutional litigators in the country and conducts hundreds of media interviews each year, including television appearances on shows such as *The O'Reilly Factor, The Sean Hannity Show, Anderson Cooper 360, The Glenn Beck Show, Good Morning America, The Today Show, Fox & Friends,* and many more.

Mat has authored hundreds of articles and has written 11 books, including *Eternal Vigilance: Knowing and Protecting Your Religious Freedom, Take Back America,* and *Same-Sex Marriage: Putting Every Household at Risk.*

Mat is married to Liberty Counsel's President, Anita Staver.

# ABOUT LIBERTY COUNSEL

L iberty Counsel is a nonprofit civil liberties education and legal defense organization established to preserve religious freedom. Founded in 1989 by Mathew D. Staver and Anita L. Staver, Liberty Counsel accomplishes its purpose in a twofold manner: through education and legal defense.

Liberty Counsel produces many aids to educate in matters of religious liberty. *The Liberator* is a monthly newsletter reviewing various religious liberty, free speech, and pro-family issues throughout the nation. The *Liberty Alert* is Liberty Counsel's periodic email newsletter. *Freedom's Call* is a two-minute daily radio program produced by Liberty Counsel providing education in First Amendment religious liberties. *Faith and Freedom* is a fifteen-minute daily radio program dedicated to religious liberty, free speech, and pro-family matters. *Law and Justice* is a weekly thirty-minute television program. Many of these resources may be obtained on our website — www.LC.org.

Liberty Counsel has produced many brochures, books, tapes, and articles outlining various aspects of religious liberty. Most of the cases in which Liberty Counsel is involved resolve through education, either by a telephone call, informative literature, or letters. Many individuals and public officials are ignorant and misinformed regarding the First Amendment. Religious and free speech rights are often restricted or lost because of ignorance.

Unfortunately, education will not solve all religious liberty issues. Some individuals are hostile and bigoted toward religion. If education does not resolve the issue, Liberty Counsel aggressively fights for religious liberty in the courtroom. Liberty Counsel represents individuals whose religious liberties are infringed and defends entities against those trying to restrict religious liberty. Liberty Counsel attorneys frequently argue cases throughout the country, including the United States Supreme Court.

Liberty Counsel is a nonprofit, tax-exempt corporation dependent upon public financial support. Contributions to Liberty Counsel are tax-deductible. For information about Liberty Counsel, or to make tax-deductible contributions, please write or call:

**Liberty Counsel**
P.O. Box 540774
Orlando, Florida 32854

(800) 671-1776 — Toll Free
(407) 875-0770 — Fax

**www.LC.org** — Website

**liberty@LC.org** — Email